P9-AGR-339

1000 ARCHITECTURAL DETAILS

1000 ARCHITECTURAL DETAILS
A Selection of the World's Most Interesting Building Elements

Àlex Sánchez Vidiella
Julio Fajardo Herrero
Sergi Costa Duran

FIREFLY BOOKS

A FIREFLY BOOK

This paperback edition published by Firefly Books Ltd. 2017

Copyright © 2010 Loft Publications

All rights reserved. No part of this publication may be reproduced, stored in a retrieval system, or transmitted in any form or by any means, electronic, mechanical, photocopying, recording or otherwise, without the prior written permission of the Publisher.

First printing

Publisher Cataloging-in-Publication Data (U.S.)

Names: Sánchez Vidiella, Àlex, author. | Fajardo Herrero, Julio, author. | Costa Duran, Sergi, author.
Title: 1000 Architectural Details : A Selection of the World's Most Interesting Building Elements / Àlex Sánchez Vidiella, Julio Fajardo Herrero, Sergi Costa Duran.
Description: Richmond Hill, Ontario, Canada : Firefly Books, 2017. | Previous edition published 2010. | Summary: An illustrated guide to interior and exterior design details with captions under each.
Identifiers: ISBN 978-1-77085-915-9 (soft cover)
Subjects: LCSH: Architecture – Details. | Architectural design. | BISAC: ARCHITECTURE / Methods & Materials.
Classification: LCC NA2850.S263 |DDC 728 – dc23

Library and Archives Canada Cataloguing in Publication

Sánchez Vidiella, Àlex, author
 1000 architectural details : a selection of the world's most interesting building elements / Àlex Sánchez Vidiella, Julio Fajardo, Sergi Costa Duran.
Previously published: 2010.
ISBN 978-1-77085-915-9 (softcover)
 1. Architecture, Modern–21st century–Pictorial works. I. Fajardo Herrero, Julio, 1979-, author II. Costa Duran, Sergi, author III. Title. IV. Title: One thousand architectural details.
NA687.V54 2017   724'.7   C2017-902202-4

Published in the United States by
Firefly Books (U.S.) Inc.
P.O. Box 1338, Ellicott Station
Buffalo, New York 14205

Published in Canada by
Firefly Books Ltd.
50 Staples Avenue, Unit 1
Richmond Hill, ON
Canada L4B 0A7

Cover Design: Maria Eugenia Castell
Printed in China

1000 Architectural Details was developed by
Loft Publications, S.L.
Via Laietana, 32, 4º, of. 92
08003 Barcelona, Spain
T +34 932 688 088
F +34 932 687 073
loft@loftpublications.com
www.loftpublications.com

Editorial coordinator:
Simone K. Schleifer

Assistant to editorial coordination:
Aitana Lleonart

Editors and text:
Àlex Sánchez Vidiella, Julio Fajardo Herrero, Sergi Costa Duran

Art director:
Mireia Casanovas Soley

Design and layout coordination:
Claudia Martínez Alonso

Layout:
Guillermo Pfaff Puigmartí

Attempts have been made to identify and contact copyright owners. Errors or omissions will be corrected in future editions.

INDEX

INTRODUCTION

This book offers a visual and theoretical analysis of the role of detail in contemporary architecture. *1,000 Architectural Details* showcases the various elements that feature in the construction of projects. The constructive details are shown through photography and drawings (floors, elevations, sections, axonometrics, sketches, etc.) that, together with a description, clarify the elements for the reader. The details have been grouped together in 15 chapters that reflect the different typical traits of current architecture.

Conceptually, the book begins with visual representations of the structures. This section includes a chapter on columns and beams as primary architectural elements. Structures that are designed to carry out different functions, columns and beams support a load, withstand exterior forces, maintain form and protect the more delicate parts. Here, a varied collection of these horizontal and vertical details are detailed.

The section following surveys façades. Since the dawn of architecture, the façade has been the object of special design attention. This exterior perimeter is the architectural presentation and the face of any construction. Wooden, stone, glass, concrete and metal façades are presented in several examples. There has been a focus on synthetic and hybrid façades (two or more materials) as an example of new contemporary architecture. The double façades — a second layer behind the first — and transparent façades or façades with lighting are the last projects included in this large group.

Roofs and decks have their own chapter. Architects use a wide range of materials that allow them to create works of art from these constructive elements that protect buildings from above.

Staircases, handrails, banisters, elevators, ramps, bridges, footbridges and walkways make up the group called Horizontal and Vertical Connections. These details connect spaces located on different levels. For example, bridges are designed to traverse an obstacle in such a way that they resist forces to which they are subjected. Although bridges must perform the function of supporting a load, this does not preclude them from being real decorative filigree-like elements.

In the construction process of a project the finishes must be taken into consideration. These details offer a wide range of possibilities and made from a variety of materials. Wood is used for its resistance to compression but above all as a decorative element. Stone has been used since the beginning of time in floors, walls, façades, etc. Concrete, one of the main materials used in constructing buildings, is prized for its excellent resistance to compression. Also, the use of reinforced concrete — concrete that steel rods have been added to — is popular. Synthetic and metal finishes such as steel (traction-resistant), aluminum, copper, etc. are commonly used in contemporary architecture. Finally, the vitreous elements (ceramic and porcelain) are used in paving pools and baths. The use of color is myriad, and very important, both in interior and exterior finishes. Color defines the artistic style of any construction.

In the Framework and Glasswork group, examples of doors, windows, skylights, fanlights, slats, fences and garden entrances are given. Crystal and glass are used interchangeably in architecture. Broadly speaking, the major difference between them is their lead content. A 4% or less lead content is called glass; greater than 4% is called crystal. In any case, they are used for their optical properties and their excellent chemical stability.

For decades, wrought iron has been only been marginally used in construction; currently its application is exclusively decorative or secondary.

The Installations, which include chimneys, stoves, climate control and acoustic insulators, are some of the details that have most evolved within the sphere of architecture, construction and design. There are a large number of companies that specialize in designing these types of installations. They are elements where functionality and aesthetics go hand in hand.

One of the most significant aspects in the creative process of a project is the lighting. This detail, used both outside and inside, has evolved with the development of technologies. New techniques, along with automated or hi-tech elements applied to architecture also are widely represented in this book.

Another chapter includes storage, bathroom decor, halls and waiting rooms. These design and architecture details are the final touches and their use generally depends on the building.

From the 1980s, sustainable and ecological architecture has becoming massively popular. This is owing to society's awareness of the effects of human activity on environmental resources. In this sense, technology is applied to architecture and it is dealt with in the chapters on sustainability, recycling and prefabricated material. Natural and sculptural elements also form part of the architectural details. Pools and water features are included in a chapter where the manipulation and use of this liquid is the focal point.

The book ends with a chapter dedicated to gardens and landscaping. The balance of soil, water and vegetation are the main characteristics of landscape architecture. Light and color have been added to this type of architecture to reflect the modern style of gardening.

0001

0002

0003

0004

0001 The support columns in this convention center lean out through the façade to become its main decorative feature. They also stretch out beyond the volume of the building to support different projecting elements.

0002 In addition to serving as supports for the upper level, half of the columns in the foyer of this shopping mall are decorative features. At a point midway to the beams, they are shaped into unusual angles and feature very original twisting.

0003 The unique Y-shaped metallic columns that support the canopies of this airport are an important decorative element of the building's façade, and are erected at slanting angles so that the canopy rises on the outside edge.

0004 The design of this pair of columns, as well as the right-hand wall, is the negative image of the features of the orange wall at the back, which is the focal point of this waiting room.

0006

007

0008

0005 The façade of this building has an unusual feature: one of the corners is open, creating space for balconies, and in place of perimeter walls, there are cylindrical columns supporting the weight of the floors.

0006 This huge central column is covered in a grid of prefabricated curved concrete panels, which is homologous with the layout of the beams supporting the roof and the square skylights that form the roof.

0007 On the main terrace of this family home, there is a robust, cylindrical column constructed from unfinished curved steel, with a rusted look. The same design is used on the other façades of the building.

0008 The columns not only support the roof, but also emphasize the effect that the house is "floating" on the Infinity pool surrounding the building. These wide, stylized columns were designed in the minimalist style dominating the house.

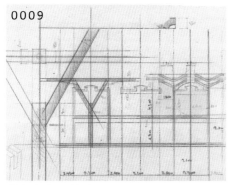

0009

Design development drawing

0010

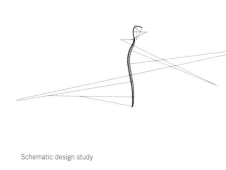

Schematic design study

0011

0012

0013

0014

7

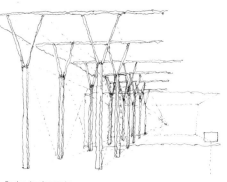

Design developments

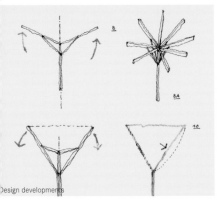

Design developments

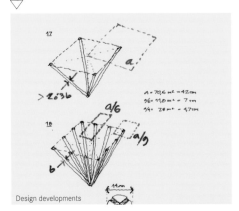

Design developments

0009 For the Modern Art Museum of Fort Worth, Tadao Ando constructed huge columns that support a roof that projects out, away from the main structure of the building.

0010 The architect Renzo Piano designed the columns and the roof of Kansai International Airport, gathering inspiration from the internal airflows. The columns bend when they reach the roof, to act as support beams.

0011 The curious shape of these exterior columns means that they have been arranged in V-shaped pairs, with an attractive metal covering. This layout only applies to the columns in front of the building; the supporting columns are completely vertical.

0012 The spectacular curved façade of this building is supported by a double metallic V-shaped pillar, which opens out towards the top and rests on a concrete plinth for stability.

0013 The cylindrical columns supporting the projection of this office block are clad in molded aluminum sheets, which protects them from the weather and possible acts of vandalism.

0014 Two enormous circular columns preside over the central patio of the Caja de Granada building, designed by the architect Alberto Campo Baeza. The design resembles a huge box of natural light constructed using large blocks of stone and glass.

0015 By using large pillars with several columns in the shape of branches emerging from them, the architects wanted to create an artificial representation of a typical Columbian rainforest tree inside the Columbia Pavilion of the Hannover Expo 2000.

0016 The false ceiling of this hall is in line with the edge of the central column, while on the other side of this separating element, the ceiling is a different height. And so, an insurmountable element becomes a divider between spaces.

0017 This impressive vestibule, the work of a Japanese architect, features a solid frame of wooden beams that hold up the roof and make possible the large expanse of the living area and high ceilings. A series of different sized beams are assembled in intricate patterns without visible anchoring.

0018 In this refurbishment project by the Martin Despang studio of architects, the wooden beams that supported the walls in the old layout have been converted into decorative elements in this semi-outdoor space, having been freed from the weight of stone and cement.

0019 A choice was made with this dwelling not to cover the industrial-look metal beams holding up the upper level of this loft. In fact, when painted a plain gray color, they become a significant decorative feature for this interior.

0020 This simple typically Scandinavian-style house features four crossbeams reinforced with diagonal struts supporting the wooden platform that is the upper level. This frame encouraged the designers to turn wood into the unquestionable star of the interior.

0021 The beam structure holding up the roof of this church becomes the leitmotif of the project and allusion is made to them in other parts of the volume. A series of triangular beams rise from the ground to connect with the crossbeams in the gabled roof, supporting part of its weight.

0022 In this small and simple residence, a simple succession of wooden pillars support a lattice of crossbeams on which the upper level rests. The same structure is used to form a canopy to protect the main entrance of the house from the rain.

0023 The unique feature of Madrid-Barajas airport is that the building's skeleton is on display. The Y-shaped pillars support the ends of the main beams. Each structural unit is made up of concrete beams creating reticula.

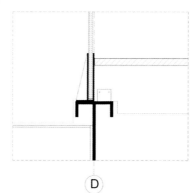

D

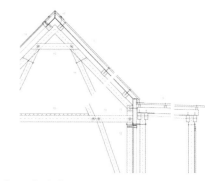

Construction details

Construction details

021

0022

0023

▷

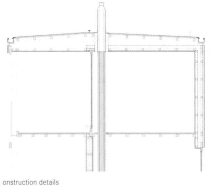

7

▷

onstruction details

Axonometric projection

0024 It is becoming increasingly common for architecture to imitate natural free-form shapes. In this image, the beams supporting the roof and creating the gallery space appear like a whale's ribcage forming pillars at the highest point.

0025 The image shows in detail the simple anchoring system fixing the side beams to the crossbeam on the roof of this public building. The white finish on all of the surfaces creates a lovely feeling of continuity.

0026 The beams of this structure form a framework of polyhedron-shaped structures that create a multi-layered effect both inside and out. They are made of wood and steel in the form of metal rings and extendable pipes. These materials blend in perfectly with the natural surroundings.

0027 Wooden beams reminiscent of the olden days, were restored to blend in with an urban lifestyle, represented by the new flooring. By doing this, the architects wanted to conserve the materials as well as the look of the original building.

0024

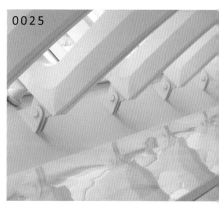

0025

0026

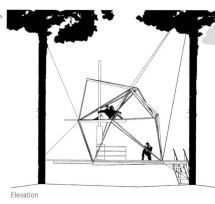

Elevation

0027

028

0029

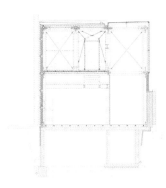

Detailed section

Suspended steel frame

030

0031

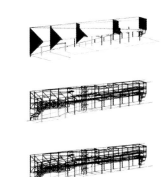

Axonometric projection

0028 The original roof of this building was completely removed, although the timber planks and beams were conserved. These were treated so as to keep them in their natural state and were reused for the building the new roof.

0029 A structure of wooden and steel beams was created to statically stabilize the annex of this house, which was built at the start of the 20th century. In this way, a new 283-cubic-foot cube was erected, giving the building more space and natural light.

0030 An architects' studio has been installed in this former dark garage space. The central post of the structure has been removed and a horizontal iron beam inserted. This large beam, which supports the roof, is painted orange to make it stand out as the main element of the installation.

0031 This project was a former industrial building, which retains the essence of the original structure: a long, rectangular shaped construction on three floors. Its most striking features are the structure of large steel beams supporting the building and enabling the façade to be glazed.

0032 The façade of this residence is clad with an 0.7-inch layer of black-stained plywood (47 × 35-inch panels), with the panels overlapping over a pine wood frame.

0033 The continuously curved façade of this spa has a façade covered in thin pine wood strips, connecting the building with its natural surroundings and giving it the appearance of a large sauna.

0034 The plywood panels cladding the entire surface of the façade of this building are overlapped and somewhat sloping at the bottom, in the way that shingles are laid on a gabled roof.

0035 Rectangular panels are a common element in Kengo Kuma's work. He has also used them in other projects in materials such as stone. Creating a somewhat broken checkerboard, the pattern of missing panels allows light to enter the building.

0032

0033

0034

0035

036

0037

0038

Construction detail

0039

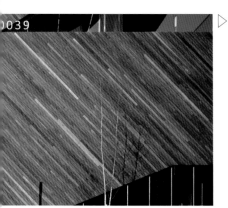

0036 For the architects of this residential development called Villa 6, the simple façade turns the building into a type of contemporary stable. The vertical wooden strips are separated enough to allow the exterior to be illuminated at night by the interior lights.

0037 The façade of this nursery school, designed by Martin Despang, is constructed with TMT (thermally modified wood) which has a very low environmental impact because it does not come from the felling of large trees. Its installation is remarkable in that it has simple fixings and a light structure, based on vertical slats.

0038 This set of buildings features a visually striking skin. The façades are clad in wooden panels, which in turn are covered with protective glass sheets to give them a truly eye-catching sheen.

0039 This building is designed as a folding screen between two gardens, located to the north and the south. One of the faces is cement and the other has a striped facing of diagonal wooden strips.

0040 Here, the work of the architects was focused on preserving the functional wood qualities of the construction. The cabin is made entirely from different types of wood. The combination of the old restored wood and new manufacture is perfect.

0041 The architecture of this church reminds us of a Finnish forest: an image of nature and spirituality. This is achieved through constructing a wooden façade. The wood has been treated and presented traditionally.

0042 On the terraced roof of a building, a student beautician wanted to install a beauty salon in the center of Tokyo. In order to do so, the Japanese architects Mount Fuji Architects used wood for this new façade. Therefore, they tried to create a new regular and heterogeneous architectural landscape.

0043 An artist couple wanted a studio-home on an existing basement in a landscaped piece of land. To cut costs, the different spaces were built with prefabricated wooden elements. On the façade treated pine wood was used that perfectly fits in with the surroundings.

0044 The façade, windows and roof have been ornamented with different types of wood that evoke the previous piece of work. This contrasts with the reinforced concrete, the greenish natural wooden slabs and the unworked dry stone that form the rest of the construction.

0045 This mountain refuge was designed as a simple wooden construction. Pinewood is the main material used in the construction. The façade has been painted a dark color to blend with the surrounding pine forest.

0040

0041

0042

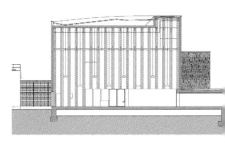

Cross section

0043

0044

0045

Front elevation

0046 This family home is made from a volume of wood on top of a concrete base. The façade is totally cove-red in wood, which facilitates the installation of large sliding windows. The wood is elegantly treated and carved.

0047 The façades and the walls of the interior of this building are clad with plywood. In the terrace and the entrance, wood has also been used but merbau wood has been used in these instances.

0048 Fir wood has been used for the façade of this apartment block located in Solsiden, Norway. Fir and oak wood have been used on the floors and walls of the rooms in the different units.

0049 On a mountainside a block of homes are being built in a 10-storey building. These houses with a cas-cade of garden terraces have façades made from woo-den slats that gives the building a sense of uniformity.

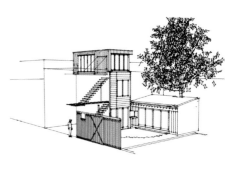

Sketch

0050 This metal building has been basically covered with wood. The horizontal, vertical and perpendicular arrangement of the different sheets gives the façade a characteristic and original design. The house has a deck on top also made from wood.

0051 The construction of this building is rectangular and it was done in mahogany wood. It was built on an old cherry orchard in Japan in the Datun Mountains. This elevation in the land means that water does not flood the interior. The wood is secured with a structure that protects it from the frequent typhoons and earthquakes.

0052 Two additions were built in wood and glass and added to an existing home. Different treated wood was used than the wood used in the main home. The two additions are the parents' room and the games room for the children.

0053 This modern and original home is protected by the wooden bark that covers it. Large slats have been used to create this look. One of the ends is perforated to create the entrance to the house.

0054 The architects decided to create this wooden cabin to establish a discreet relationship with the natural environment. In order to do so, they adopted the traditional Chilean constructions as a design. The wooden clad walls and ceiling create a continuous layer.

0055 The wood used on the façade was painted a silver-grey color, establishing a harmonious communication with the rest of the buildings that surrounds it. There is also a direct relationship with the surrounding stone walls. The wood allows for small openings that serve as windows in the façade.

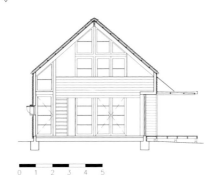

0   1   2   3   4   5

Section

0056

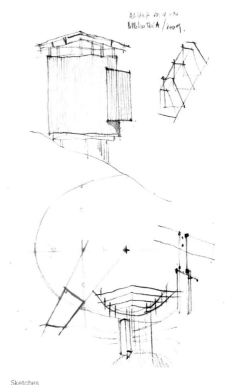

Sketches

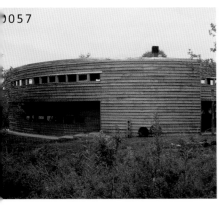

0057

0058

0059

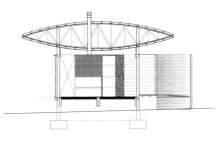

Section

0056 This library was designed as an annex of the main house, in spite of being connected to it visually and formally. The structure is made from wood and rests upon posts. The use of wood for the façade establishes a better connection with the environment that surrounds it.

0057 The prominent feature of this home is the wood in its natural state, used throughout the building. Elaborate and complex woodwork is visible on the windowsill, blinds and latticework. This structure gives the house a rustic feel.

0058 The home is designed as a wooden canopy that protects the construction of one space. The structure, basically erected in wood, is designed to support the weight of the snow. The wooden decking allows us to create an undulating design on the façade.

0059 The façade of the main body that shapes this project was built with an exterior plywood paneling. This material is used because it is economical and easy to assemble.

0060

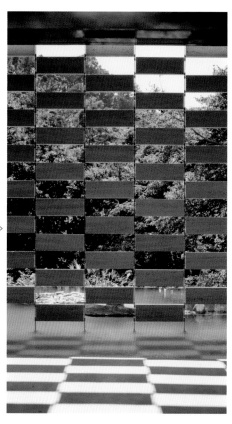

0061

0062

0063

0064

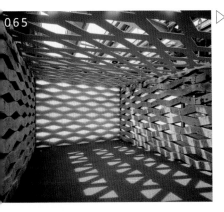

0060 This cultural center located in Galicia, Spain, features a cladding normally used on roofs: rectangular slate tiles. They are arranged vertically instead of in the traditional, overlapped style common to many villages in the area.

0061 This residence has two strongly marked volumes containing the interior spaces. It is clad almost in its entirety with slate panels in different shades. This cladding perfectly offsets the white paving around the swimming pool and completely hides the front door and entrance to the garage.

0062 This project fills a volume with holes, both as the result of the shape of the balconies and the layout of walls. The voids and 1.2-inch-thick rectangular travertine marble panels form a spectacular checkerboard held up by longitudinal steel bars.

0063 The spaces in this country house are laid out along a rectangular pool and adjoin a stone wall running north-south following the line of the pool. The combination of wood and stone covering walls and floors — material chosen for their visual, textural, and acoustic qualities — connect the house with the surrounding landscape.

0064 The uneven relief achieved with these limestone walls makes them a decorative feature for these rustic but contemporary interiors.

0065 This project demonstrates a diagonal construction system where the stones are positioned in pairs and interwoven like wicker inside a steel frame. What is really special about the result is that the stone is not only a material that is applied or used as cladding, but is a structural part of the walls.

0066 With ventilated façades clad in travertine marble, this house is a striking combination of basic traditional materials like stone and glass arranged over a cutting-edge structural frame. With a simple rectangle as a starting point, the design was developed into numerous spaces with very pronounced angles.

0067 The ruins of an old country house with a privileged location between a river and a eucalyptus forest was the starting point for this reconstruction more than remodeling project. Use was made of the original positioning of the stone walls.

0068 By integrating the new work with the thick granite outer walls, past and present were combined in the final result. The new main volume, a long rectangle with a white frame, overlooks the site through a wide floor-to-ceiling window.

0069 This cemetery features two basic materials: stone facings and brickwork lined with white mortar. The rough and many-hued stone was positioned with the intention of resembling a pixel map.

0070 A design competition held by Dalski Stone inspired this display for their stone. The winning design is noteworthy for its three-dimensional structure and the use of rare varieties of stone, such as Asian sandstones, featuring ones in light green and chocolate brown, among others.

0071 Solid and even surfaces guarantee strength for this streetcar stop, as well as the safety of its users. Information panels are embedded in the stone from different quarries, which results in a stylized design that protects the entire structure from vandalism and inclement weather.

0068

▽

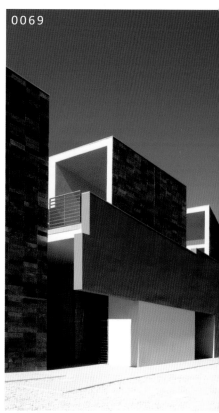

0069

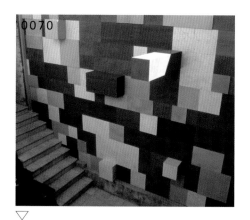

0070

▽

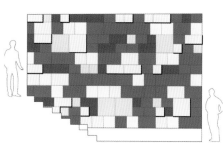

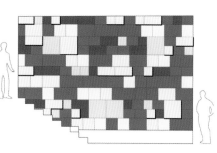

Side elevation

0071

0072

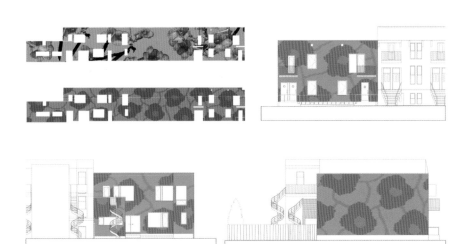

Side elevations

0073

0074

0075

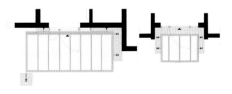

Door section

0072 In this centennial home, near Montreal, the façades were renovated; they were cleaned to be subsequently visually revived. The final façade design was a floral inspiration using colored bricks, evoking painted wallpaper.

0073 The façade of this French residence is constructed under a base of rough concrete filled with local stone. These stones come from small walls built by farmers. On the upper levels there is a brickwork structure over which there are wooden slats.

0074 The design of the exterior walls of this doorway required a low cost configuration that ensures the façade was protected against vandalism. The solution, inserting untreated stone pebbles in wire cages has a great visual presence, in addition to providing strength.

0075 In this project, the architects wanted to combine the traditional architectural of the site through using brick on the outside, with a modern design in the interior spaces. As a result, local stone was used on the exterior.

0076

0077

0078

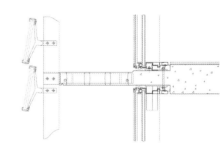

Façade construction detail

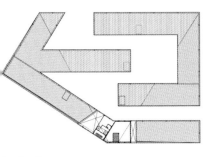

General layout

0080

0082

0076 DecorFlou satin-finished glass sheets by Omnidecor offer a perfect balance between opacity and transparency, with an unbeatable light diffusion effect that makes them ideal for use in façades of buildings with little interior lighting.

0077 The façade of this building is like a three-dimensional checkerboard. The cubic shapes of the building and its projections are mirrored in the grid supporting the glass panels.

0078 The façade of this embassy features a succession of inclined transparent glass slats resembling Venetian blinds. However, being clear, they do not filter light. Their purpose is purely decorative, although they do favor proper ventilation.

0079 The façades of this office complex designed by UNStudio are completely clad in rectangular glass sheets. What makes them special is their layer of multicolored pigment, which changes color depending on solar incidence and the brightness of the day.

0080 Modern construction materials, particularly light metal structures, enable glass façades to be installed in unconventional shapes, like this building which is in the same curved shape as the sail of a boat.

0081 The wooden façade of this residence is protected by a layer of glass sheets. Held up by simple metal fasteners similar to those used on some photo frames, the thin acid-etched glass sheets are positioned in horizontal bands.

0082 This Herzog & De Meuron project is an example of the results of close collaboration between architects and suppliers of materials. Thanks to the involvement of Cricursa, a spectacular design using curved glass has been created on the façade, which has undoubtedly become the project's distinguishing feature.

0083 One of the most spectacular buildings in Federation Square in Melbourne, Australia, is the Atrio, located between the National Gallery of Victoria and the Australian Center for the Moving Image. Its remarkable glass, steel and zinc structure in the form of geometric shapes lets onlookers see inside from the square outside.

0084 This museum, located in Akron, Ohio, is divided into three bodies, one of which is called The Glass Pavilion. The large façade is glazed and its dimensions allow an interior climate control system that uses very little artificial energy.

0085 The architects decided to set up a dialogue between the building and the huge mosaic of 1,312 × 262 feet located in the central square. The geometric shapes of the work of Byron Gálvez visually deconstruct the reflective glass panels on the façade of the Teatro-Auditorio Gota de Plata located at a height of 82 feet.

0086 A curvilinear glass curtain falls organically over the façade of this New York apartment building. The curtain is comprised of 1-inch thick insulating glass sheets tinted blue-green, some of which are curved.

0083

0084

0085

0086

Three-dimensional representation

0088

089

0090

0087 A translucent veil of acid-etched glass stamped with abstract patterns hangs over the heavy stone volume of this building. Its color is light during the day, but a lighting system turns this glass layer into a multicolored display at night.

0088 The façade of this house was the inspiration for this project. A glass frontage runs from end to end without any frame except for the floor and the ceiling. This feature is particularly eye-catching owing to the absence of elements that cover, for example, the interior of the bathroom.

0089 From the interior, uninterrupted floor to ceiling glass affords panoramic views. However, from the outside the sheets of glass have an effect like the tinted glass on cars, and act like a mirror.

0090 Erick van Egeerat tends to put spectacular clear façades on his buildings. For this town hall building he designed a wavy skin with square, cloud-patterned sheets.

0091

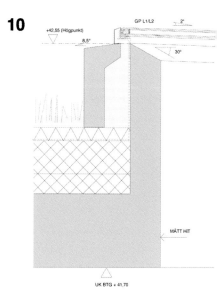

10

Construction detail

0091 The thick unrendered concrete outer walls of this house have a metal border at the top. This band marks the start of the roof and acts as a parapet.

0092 The façade of this funeral home is clad in 3.2 × 3.2 foot precast concrete panels with a relief of concentric squares. This pattern gives depth to the outer face of the building while maintaining an appropriately somber mood.

0093 This façade is covered in slightly sloping prefabricated concrete panels, covering the building in an interesting series of gills.

0094 The striking façade of this building overlays the typical glass and steel grid with a pattern of precast concrete panels to create a kind of architectural ribbing, a mesh of incredibly decorative diamonds.

0095 Concrete has been chosen for this school: a material which was misused in the 1970s but which continues to have great advantages in terms of thermal insulation, shade and structural pillars.

0096 The concrete columns and crossbeams of the structure of this commercial building extend beyond the interior spaces, forming an exoskeleton that is somewhat raw but makes a great architectural statement and benefits from the slightly industrial look of the rest of the complex.

0097 El Ala (the wing) is one of the architectural highlights of the Tenerife Auditorium. It is built in raw concrete and over a triangular base. It rises from the rear of the auditorium, and rests on the apex to reach a height of 190 feet.

0092

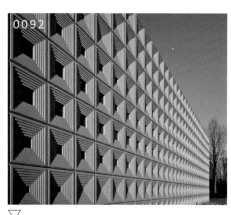

0093

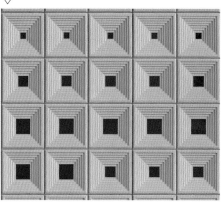

0094

0095

0096

0097

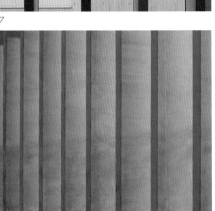

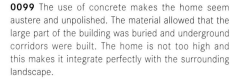

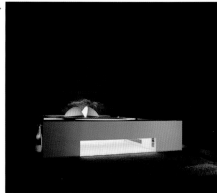

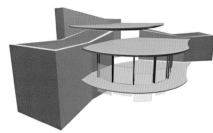

Three-dimensional representation

0098 The architects treated the concrete to give a sandy aspect to the main façade. Color and texture are the elements that form these irregular walls and make the Baptist Church in Sendai stand out from the other adjoining buildings.

0099 The use of concrete makes the home seem austere and unpolished. The material allowed that the large part of the building was buried and underground corridors were built. The home is not too high and this makes it integrate perfectly with the surrounding landscape.

0100 The façade of this new church in Rijsenhout, in The Netherlands, is clad with treated concrete. This type of treatment that is applied to the façade, gives it a stone look that at the same time provides the façade with a sober, modern and dynamic look.

0101 The use of concrete in the façades provides a sense of continuity and sobriety to the building just as the owner asked of the architects. To emphasize this wish they have used steel and glass as constructive materials.

0102 The white painted concrete of this mosque allowed the architects to make large openings in the façade leaving the construction exposed to the elements. Therefore large openings were created in the dome, which were protected with large circular windows and large windows on the two sides.

0103 The structure of this building was built in concrete. The architects did not cover the façade so as to lend it an austere and unfinished aspect. The project was designed as a single house, for this reason each of the three volumes has its own function.

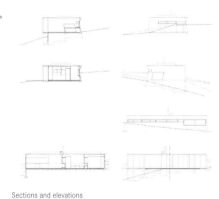

Sections and elevations

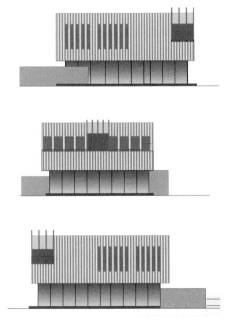

Side elevations

0104 To carry out this complex project, the architects chose concrete as it constituted the material that best resembles the art of the sculptor Jorge Yazpik. Concrete is a moldable, versatile, changeable material, and it perfectly combines with other materials, such as stone and wood.

0105 The owners' directives were twofold: low-cost, and minimum ecological impact. To achieve these two objectives the architects used concrete as a economical material and because it is easily maintained, in addition to the fact that it perfectly fits in the surroundings.

0106 When this project was suggested, the main objective was to build a house that left the cliff intact but at the same time was comfortable for its users. The structure of the house is made from two parallelogram-shaped volumes that cross at a point that gives rise to the patio. These shapes are built from silver-painted concrete.

0107 The architect wanted to put across the idea of an unfinished piece of work. In order to do so, concrete was used to build a solid corbel. In addition, he used different types of stone that along with the concrete give a deliberate rough and unfinished look.

0108 The leitmotif of this Melbourne home is to reflect that its owners are in the concrete business. To demonstrate this, concrete was used as the most representative material. For example, exposed concrete was used on the upper level.

0109 The stability of this daring construction was guaranteed by an elaborate structure of concrete, steel and wood. This enabled the architect to create three storeys, with the lower level partially sunk into the cliff. The concrete also allowed the architects to create the façades as if they were carved.

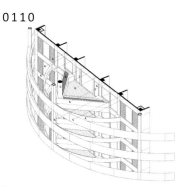
0110

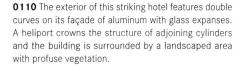
Façade construction detail

0110 The exterior of this striking hotel features double curves on its façade of aluminum with glass expanses. A heliport crowns the structure of adjoining cylinders and the building is surrounded by a landscaped area with profuse vegetation.

0111 A former electrical substation dating from 1907 forms the core structure of this new museum, to which Daniel Libeskind has added a protective layer of over 3,000 blue steel panels. This new skin seems to change its color and intensity depending on the solar incidence.

0112 The perforated aluminum panels on the façade of this Rotterdam parking garage filter sunlight and also turn the building into a source of artificial illumination at night.

0111

0112

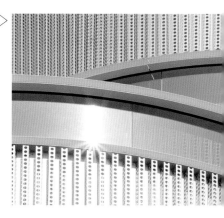

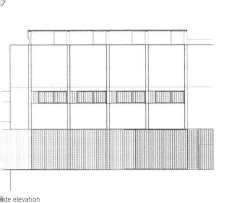

ide elevation

0113 This "floating" residential building's originality is found to a large degree in its varied façade, the result of using different types of metal cladding. There is abundant use of large windows and of corrugated metal sheeting painted in bright colors.

0114 The fixed, slightly curved mesh sunblinds protect the entrances to the different dwellings in this building from excess solar incidence. From the outside, these visual barriers give the building personality and are its distinguishing feature.

0115 The Denver Art Museum, a work by Daniel Libeskind, features a façade entirely clad in titanium panels. This material has enjoyed widespread popularity for public buildings since Frank Gehry began to use it in his designs.

0116

Perspective view

0117

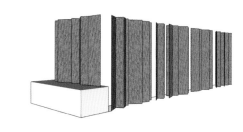

Schematic drawing

0118

0119

Side elevation

0116 The sculptural shape of this UNStudio designed theater in Lelystad, Netherlands, comes from the combination of oblique planes clad with electric orange perforated metal sheets.

0117 The land around this residence is intelligently fenced off by a broken succession of vertical panels of 5.9-inch-thick weathering steel that form wedges in different directions and allow a certain amount of light to pass from one side to the other.

0118 Entirely clad in square aluminum panels, the different shades of gray on this windowless industrial building were achieved by separating or joining the points stamped with ornamental motifs on the surface of each panel.

0119 The originality of this house lies in the way the aluminum panels of the façade cladding were assembled. Positioned like shingles, the pattern they form resembles that of a brick building, and they appear to be a modernized version of bricks.

0120 Sculpted in the shape of an opening book, this building becomes a "letter maze", clad in spice colored aluminum, which greatly links it to the colors of the land. The structure's impact comes mainly from the visual continuity of its shapes.

0121 The metal frame of this simple residence is completely clad with 0.08-inch-thick aluminum sheets. The façade sheets are flat, while those on the gabled roof are corrugated for relief.

0120

0121

0123

0122 Most of the façade of this Philadelphia residential building is clad in gray aluminum panels. This cladding beautifully offsets the areas of black plaster, although both zones never come in contact.

0123 Panels of corrugated sheet metal are not only useful for covering drab-looking industrial buildings. If the sheet of aluminum is flexible enough, it can also be curved and produce truly beautiful results.

0124 The matt finish aluminum panels covering this industrial building are assembled in such a way that each one is never at the same height as the one next to it, like the classic layout of traditional brick walls.

0125 The façade of the headquarters of this mechanical engineering firm features a striking checkerboard pattern made of aluminum sheets stamped with ornamental circle motifs. The result is a bold façade that contributes to the company's corporate image.

0126 The two truncated cones featured on the structure of the new central complex of automaker BMW are covered with striped aluminum panels, which give it a sense of lightness and a very attractive relief.

0124

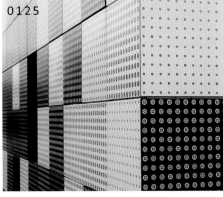

0125

0126

0127

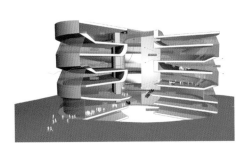

0128

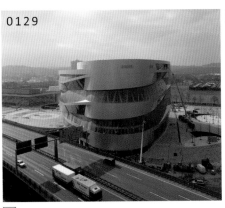

0129

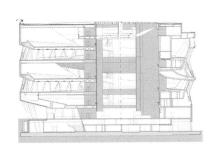

Sections

Façade construction detail

0130

0131

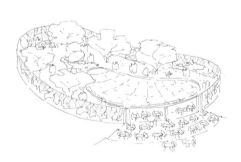

Sketch

▽

0132

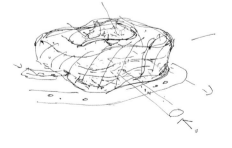

29 — 10 — 14

Exterior schematic sketch

0127 In the main façade of this building, designed by the architect Christian de Portzamparc, there are a series of glass layers containing the text of Victor Hugo on the freedom of the press, and a drawing of Plantu, the most famous illustrator of the French daily newspaper *Le Monde*.

0128 The skeleton of this theater is wrapped in a circular skin made with a PVC membrane. Tinted electric red, this material bathes the interiors in an extraordinary orange light.

0129 The Mercedes-Benz Museum, located in Stuttgart, gives the impression of floating weightlessly above the ground, despite its weight of 110,000 tons. Steel plates are used in the exterior façade and it features large windows made from 1,800 triangular plates of glass of varying sizes.

0130 The background of this building is painted a deep Yves Klein blue. During the day, the second layer of the façade is concealed by the disks installed in it, but at night the blue light shines highlighting the spherical forms.

0131 The National Gallery of Victoria, in Australia, has a south façade with a structure of grilles in a fractal arrangement that creates a changing surface. Highly malleable materials such as zinc, sandstone and glass were used to construct this façade.

0132 Limestone, concrete, stainless steel, glass, ceramic tiles and wood are the elements making up the main façade of the house. Glass is used in windows and balustrades, and stainless steel is used in supporting and load-bearing structures. These materials help minimize the house's visual impact on its setting.

0133

0134

0135

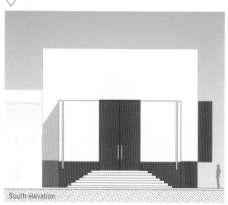

South elevation

0133 Ceramic and glass cladding have been used on this façade. The use of ceramic and porcelain cladding in façades is on the rise. Ceramics have gone from being used in flooring to a more aesthetic and practical use for covering façades.

0134 In the Spanish city of Castellón a new multifunctional cemetery has been built for all religions who require this type of service. The originality of the ensemble stems from the façade covered on the upper half with white concrete and weathered steel on the lower half.

0135 The House of Meditation in Mexico City is built from granite slabs and camaru wood. The combination of these materials with the pure and austere lines gives the house a sense of peace, both in the interior and exterior of the construction.

0136 The façade of this urban home is covered with galvanized sheets. Concrete has been used for the structure of the construction. On the Northside, large glass surfaces without visible frames dominate the work with large ventilation openings.

0137 To design the main headquarters of the company Viken Skog BA, the architects drew inspiration from building with wood and its connection with nature. On the different façades that make up the building, wood and large glass panels were used that allow the cone located in the center of the building to be seen.

0138 The façade of this building reflects the different levels with its respective spaces through the use of different materials. In this way, wood is used in the upper floors, where the rooms are; the lower floor is glazed and is home to the common areas, and the basement is made using concrete.

0136

0137

0138

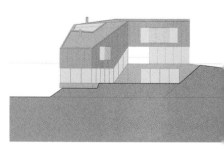

Side elevation

0139 Located in a natural surrounding, the façade of this home was built using four main materials: stone, glass, wood and steel. To integrate the project in its surroundings, typical materials from the area were used, for example local stone, which can be seen on both the façade and the interior.

0140 On the upper half of this house-studio, pinewood was used, while on the lower half cement slabs were used. The architects devised this original design for two reasons: fire protection and building physics principles.

0141 In spite of the different materials used to construct the façade, it has remained almost completely white. These materials are concrete, wood, glass and stone.

0142 White steel, undulated metal sheets, wood and stucco are all the materials used in this American home. Wood and stucco are used because they are local materials and they integrate better with the environment.

0143 In this university residence, designed by Murphy/Jahn, glass sheet and stainless steel cladding act as a screen, adding to the insulation and blocking unsightly views.

0144 The concrete façade of this building does not open directly onto the street. In the middle there is a covered space, with a gap for an emergency staircase, separated from the exterior by a wall made from large glass panels, which seems to transform the structure into a museum collection piece in a protective case.

0145 A fine translucent mesh of stainless steel covers the glass façade of this Camenzind Evolution building. This skin elegantly unfurls as it ascends, adapting to the spiral shaped building.

0146 The Agbar Tower building in Barcelona has a front façade constructed from concrete. A first skin covers the wall with a sheet of lacquered aluminum with 25 different colors in reds, blues, greens and grays. The façade has a second skin formed by layers of translucent and transparent glass.

0147 This corporate building is a horizontal three-story volume with concrete curtain walls. These are suspended and separated from the façades and are composed of glass and steel with prints in yellow tones. On one of the façades, the windows are replaced with metal panels that are perforated to filter the sunlight.

0148 Glass is the most abundant material in the east façade of this building in Berlin, where it predominates. Steel is another material that is used in the building's other façades. Wood painted in different colors forms part of a second façade.

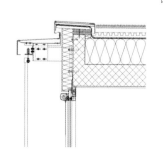

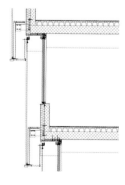

Sections

146

0147

148

0149

0149 This original façade in a Barcelona office block located in the new financial district is clad with a stainless steel metallic fabric. They have created spherical patterns in this mesh by insetting the fabric.

0150 The originality of this construction lies in the prolonged roof towards the façade in such a way that it seem to safeguard the building, while forming a double structure. The concrete and large windows are protected by wide, hard, horizontal wooden panels.

0151 The architects drew inspiration from the local traditional Norwegian cabins so that the construction would perfectly fit in with the surroundings. The façade is made from slate, wood and natural stone. Oak and varnished pine has been used.

0152 The building is the truncated cone of an elliptical plant that measures 384 × 243 feet, beveled and clad in wood. This singular double-façade gives singularity and independence to the new Barcelona skyline.

0153 The façade of this commercial building, located in the Ginza district in Tokyo, is made from steel sheets that have been filled with concrete to create a fine structure and achieve higher resistance. The exterior image presents a different typology to the abstract image on the inside.

0154 In this Australian restaurant located in the Bay of Sydney, a double-glazed façade has been voluntarily created in order to install an elongated terrace. The terrace, which is narrow and covered, doubles up as a viewpoint and occasional dining area.

0155 On this double façade, a zinc covering has been used on concrete and aluminum to create a sense of secretiveness. Inside it seeks to capture the maximum amount of light possible through the use of windows and glass directed towards the interior patios.

0156 El Patio restaurant, located in the artistic neighborhood of la Condesa, in Mexico City, has a unique façade. It has an exterior layer of folding shutters used according to the wishes of the owners, and an interior layer made up of medium-height concrete walls and the remainder windows.

0157 This is a clear example of multiple-layers on façades. In this Californian synagogue different layers has been created on the façade through the use of large windows that double up as dividers. The architects decided on this original structure to achieve natural ventilation and, above all, increased control of lighting.

0150

0151

0152

0153

0154

0155

0156

0157

Sketches

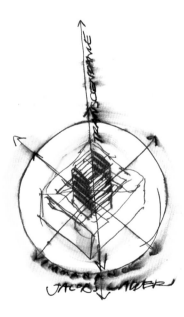

0158

0159

0160

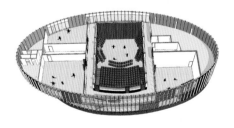

Third-floor perspective view

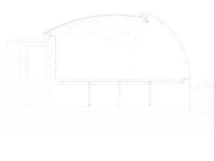

Section

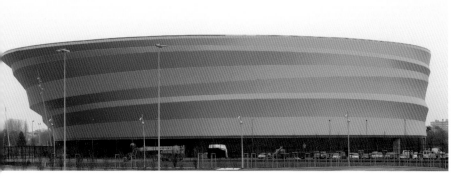

Frame construction detail

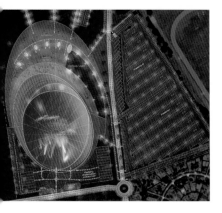

0162

163

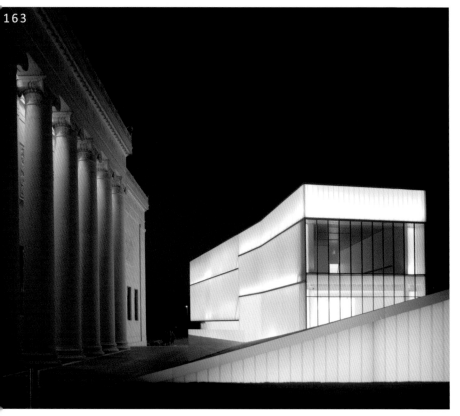

0158 The blue glass façade of this commercial center is mirrored in a canal adjoining the complex. Nighttime backlighting enhances the presence of the building and turns it into one of the most easily identifiable structures in the area.

0159 The façade of this multiple-use building, designed by Paul de Ruiter, is made with very low-cost materials, which does not take detract from the visual impact of the translucent membrane covering the entire elliptic shape of the building.

0160 This chapel is formed by two leaves, one made of steel and the other made of glass, which seem to have come up from the ground. With a lace pattern imprinted over it, the glass leaf acts as a pergola and is supported by the structure.

0161 The dynamic design of this concert venue is largely the result of the way the elliptic frame of the metal façade is fragmented and rotated at the same time, and the combination of the visual impact of the translucent skin enveloping the foyer.

0162 Transparent and open, the outer layer of this structure features a series of aluminum panels that create a rippled effect reminiscent of spirals. An LED lighting system illuminates the façade at night with different patterns.

0163 The Bloch Building is a new structure erected next to the Nelson-Atkins Museum's main building. Located in a sculpture garden, the new addition is like another piece of the collection. The architect's intention was for visitors to experience the flow of light, art, architecture, and landscape.

0164 The façade of this building by the architects Murphy/Jahn is a single shade of blue during the day, but takes on different colors at night by means of a sophisticated LED point lighting system.

0165 The 10 stories of this building are hidden behind a cement grid and shine outwardly through the small squares of the façade to create a striking magic lantern effect.

0166 An outstanding part of the design of this project was reflecting the notion of telecommunications on the façade of the building by means of an intelligent system of changing lights that, for example, offer stock market information.

0167 The façade of this building essentially functions as an advertisement, given that the LED lighting system works like a giant video screen. The result for the business established in the building – Uniqlo – is that sales have beaten expectations fourfold.

0168 This luminous box overlooks the street through a bold façade made from thin sheets of Pakistani onyx assembled between two glass panels. The façade also features PET panels with a pattern that is very similar to the onyx.

0169 This commercial building designed by the Italian architect Massimiliano Fuksas has a subtle LED light display which is not garish and which perfectly encapsulates the elegant image of the commercial brand to which it belongs: Armani.

0170 This office block located in the Spanish capital is designed by the Galán Lubascher studio of architects. Its façade, horizontally crossed by lines of LED lights, can change color at night, so that the exterior aspect of the building is lit up differently to highlight special occasions for the company.

0164

0165

0166

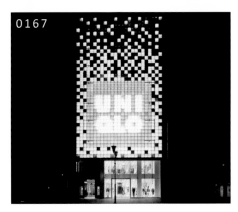
0167

0169

0170

▷

0171 This gigantic residential and leisure development designed by Steven Holl features different buildings connected by a series of walkways positioned at different levels on each volume, with no supports other than at the ends, and clad in practically unbroken glazed surfaces.

0172 The way the architects of this residence designed spaces for balconies could not have been more simple or original. They perforated a rectangular volume with a series of boxes, not unlike taking ice cubes out of an ice tray, to obtain semi-exterior spaces.

0173 Located on a site adjacent to a hillside, space is gained for this dwelling by having one of its rooms hang over the slope by means of a light wooden structure. This also affords spectacular panoramic views.

0174 The wooden projection overhanging the entrance to this house like a canopy does not only have a decorative function: it also acts as a tensioning support for the wooden frame bearing the weight of the volume.

0171

0172

0173

Floor plan

Axonometric projection

0174

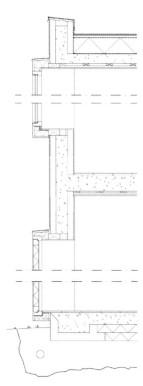

Construction details

0175 The projecting wood of the window frames in this residence not only forms a distinctive feature of the façade but also offers spaces for seats and storage in the shape of deep window sills.

0176 A system of integral custom-made formwork previously used on other projects enabled the building process for the projections on these façades not to be slowed down in the least despite their original shape. The area gained in floor space can sometimes fit a complete bedroom.

0177 The arms connecting the tops of these residential buildings are actually two-story penthouses, which contribute to the visual enclosure of the site while creating huge apertures below to open the complex out to the exterior.

0178

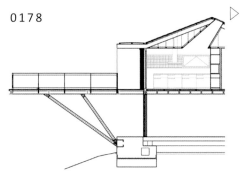

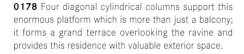
Plan and section

0180

0179

0181

0182

0178 Four diagonal cylindrical columns support this enormous platform which is more than just a balcony; it forms a grand terrace overlooking the ravine and provides this residence with valuable exterior space.

0179 The unusual shape of this site led the architects to design a building with very sharp angles. In order to do something more with the space between the cutting planes at these points, striking balconies were created, like arrowheads with which the building pierces the air.

0180 The unique wedge shape of the projections on this façade offers rooms a supplementary space that acts like an interior balcony. The face through which less light enters remains protected, and the windows overlook a more open exterior area.

0181 If this building were turned on its side, its façade would have the same outline as a step ladder. Vertically, these steps allow each balcony to have a greater panoramic view than if the façade were flat.

0182 The rings in front of each level of the façade of this building enhance its curved shape and protect the levels immediately below from excessive solar incidence. They are held up by a series of barely visible steel cables.

0183 This striking building stands out by virtue of its spectacular periscope shape. The architects decided to take advantage of its privileged setting and cantilever its cornice out to produce a long projection encased in glass, inside which an observation deck was created.

0184 This pergola-like latticed frame structure is the focal point of this building, the façade of which is a simple grid of tinted glass. More than providing shade, the projection was designed for the purely aesthetic purpose of adding volume to the building for dramatic effect.

0185 The balconies extend the corners of this building to create sinuous curves that form the outline of its façade. The metal bands enveloping them are the perfect decorative flourish to the building's design.

0186 The volume cantilevered out from this large office building is divided into two: one part is totally covered, with barely any windows breaking its façade. This is made possible because the other half is taken up by wide balconies that bathe the interior with light.

0187 The width of this building's balconies is remarkable. The cantilevered area is shared by two neighboring residences, and the two areas are separated by a partitioning panel in the same covering as the façade.

0188 This modern office building in Vilnius, Lithuania, features a west-facing, wedge-shaped cantilevered projection on its upper stories that serve as a windowed balcony and allow light into the main interior offices.

0189 Use was made of the part of the building coinciding with the chamfered street corner to create a circular projection on the highest level, which serves as an observation deck. This balcony turns the penthouse into the most privileged space in the building.

0190 The design of this office block is a reinterpretation of the traditional oriental pagoda. The curved cantilevered projections are clad in sheets of aluminum and are essentially for decoration only.

0191 The protective handrail of this balcony is divided into two parts, one metallic and one which integrates a decorative red plastic panel, fitted at the edges so as to alternate between the apartments on different floors.

0192 Bloomframe is a patented design which can help when there is a lack of space in small apartments, and at the same time provide a small outdoor space for apartments without balconies. When it is folded out, the window provides a horizontal space as a balcony: it uses a mechanism that is impressively simple.

0193 The façade of this curious building is interrupted not only by cylindrical pillars, but also by a series of projections; narrow balconies that stick out like the beginnings of walkways, protected by panels of frosted glass in the form of handrails.

0194 This terrace handrail was constructed in wrought iron with a rusted finish. It is mounted onto a closure plate fixed to the floor, which has fixings on the sides. The railings are made from solid wrought iron.

0186

0187

0188

189

0190

0191

0192

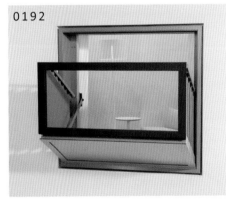

▽

0193

0194

0195

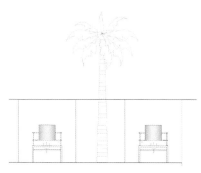

Section

0196

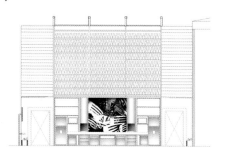

Section

0195 The need to preserve the trees in this courtyard challenged the genius of the architect, who designed an ultra-light and virtually transparent structure to cover the rooms with glass panels without blocking the entry of light.

0196 Four steel beams tilted to an angle of 50° hold up this impressive roof, modeled on the typical gabled roof but made with panels of armored glass. The views are guaranteed.

197

0198

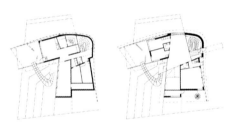

Floor plans

0199

200

ide elevation

0197 The roof of this residence is an example of a trend that has enjoyed widespread popularity in recent years: covering the roof with impermeable plastic before covering it with soil and vegetation to blend the house completely into its natural surroundings.

0198 The roof of this Finnish home is covered in an ultra-light aluminum layer. In addition to covering the house, the protection continues like a canopy over the façade, following the same curve and thermally protecting the interior with its solidity.

0199 The limited space in a place as densely populated as Japan calls for solutions like this aluminum roof, which becomes the façade of the tiny house it covers.

0200 A way was found to turn the attic of this building with a typical gabled roof into a bright, almost semi-exterior dwelling: the architect replaced most of the tiles for sloping PVC skylights, many of them folding.

0201 The roof of this house was designed making use of a typical material in industrial buildings: corrugated metal sheeting. What is striking in this case is the accentuated curve of the roof.

0202 Located in a privileged setting, this ecological hotel is another example of a green roof. Through the use of a thick synthetic insulating layer, the same grass as that surrounding the building could be sown on the roof.

0203 Looking amazingly organic, the roof of this hotel makes use of small, very shiny tiles to create angle-free and discreet mounds that coincide with the highest ceilings inside the buildings.

0204 An enormous veil with a tremendously organic aspect covers the entire foyer area like a giant transparent canopy. This wavy marquee turns the esplanade into a transition space between the interior and the exterior.

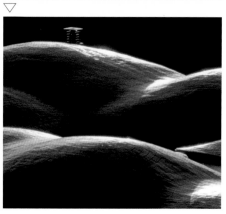

205

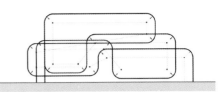

Construction detail

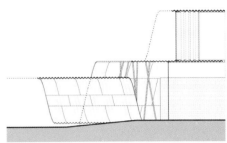

Section

206

0207

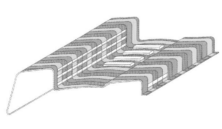

208

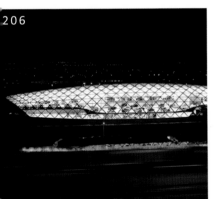

Window header and cantilevered roof section

0205 The roof of this exhibition space has actually become almost the entire structure. Corrugated metal sheeting winds down from the top of the building to give spectacular results.

0206 Roofs built using light tubular frames have enjoyed great popularity with architects of visually-striking projects. Like honeycombs – replacing hexagons with triangles – these volumes enable the slope of the roofs to be modeled at will.

0207 The harsh climate led the architects to give this research center a solid protective layer using copper panels. The result is amazingly futuristic, while also performing its thermal function to perfection.

0208 The wave-like form of this roof is particularly striking as it envelops the entire building. It acts in the same way as the traditional panel of corrugated sheet metal, except that it gives each section of relief much greater length.

0209

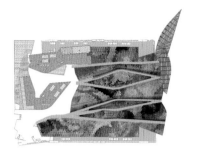

Roof plan

0210

0211

Section

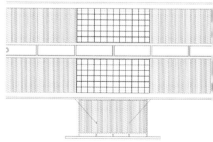

Section

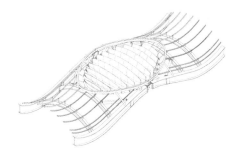

Axonometric roof detail

213

0214

Roof plan

0209 The three metal arches passing through the roof transversally also support its pull. The rest is a wave-like mantle covered with hexagonal mosaic tiles in a wide range of colors, reminiscent of the work of Antoni Gaudí.

0210 Another example of the trend to cover roofs with organic "fabric". Here the slope of the terrain seems to have been imitated when compared to typical plans produced with computer-assisted design programs.

0211 This university classroom block has the classic semicircular vaulted metal roof, but it also features two very striking innovative elements: the expansion of skylights covering the foyer, and two large crossbeams containing service pipes, which become the focal point of the project.

0212 The amazing physical properties of this roof are the result of its lightness and the way the wave shape allows its weight to be spread over such thin columns. The cladding, wood inside and metal outside, gives an elegant finish to the project.

0213 The flexibility offered by the system of metal crossbeams enables the glass sheets of this green-house to form an incredibly pronounced elliptical shape once they are fitted. The barely noticeable anchoring system for each sheet is another design feature.

0214 Infinite coating and cladding systems are com-bined in the design of this railroad terminal roof. An external aluminum layer protects the roof, which is held up by a network of tree-like columns.

0215 This redesign project by Schwarz Design, draws attention to the columns with arms that have been installed to support the impressive roof that is based on longitudinal slats. This structure highlights the openness of the interior space and achieves an attractive visual effect.

0216 The roof of this trade show venue rests over slender circular columns on cantilevered supports. The tallest columns are 39 feet in height. Each of the beams supporting the roof is 236 feet-long.

0217 The different canopies over balconies and openings of this building are overlapped like layers of mille-feuille pastry. The curved shape enables intermediate panels to be inserted between the different levels to create an almost hypnotic effect.

0218 The detail in this image shows a nexus of struts, both in the overall structure and in the cables, which support the roof of this concert hall. The cables also help to keep the canvas taut, which covers the structure in triangular shapes.

0219 The metal structure supporting this huge vaulted roof is of astounding complexity. A grid acting as a frame, a system of transversal tensioners, and another comprising arches and vertical braces share the load.

0220 The impressive roof of this shopping mall is reminiscent of the metal lacework in the skeletons of a number of late 19th century public buildings. The broad arches support the latticework of horizontal bars the glass sheets rest on.

0221 This space for agricultural fairs shares structural basics with the previous detail. However, here the it is arch spanning the vault that supports its load, leaving the sides practically free from supports.

Construction details

220

0221

Axonometric projection

Axonometric roof detail

0222 The conical and curved shapes of this handrail resemble blades of grass; they seem to be planted in the ground and gently swaying. The handrail, which is 6.6 feet long and 2.5 feet high, acts as an entrance to a swimming pool.

0223 Hoja handrail, constructed and designed by Forjas Artísticas El Francés (Belmonte, Spain). The central plant-based design, through repetition along the handrail, blends perfectly into the rural environment surrounding the residence.

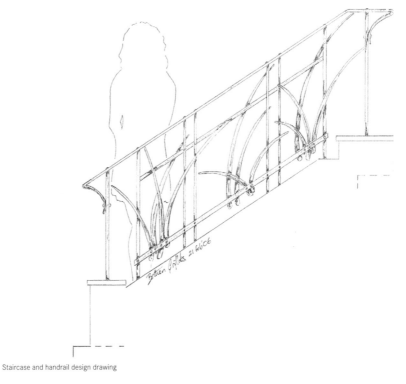

Staircase and handrail design drawing

0224 This fire escape was painted the same color as the façade so as not to create too strong a contrast, and features a circular guard at regular distances to ensure users' safety.

0225 The fire escape of this Rotterdam building was placed on the exterior, something increasingly rare and calling to mind past times. However, with an eye-catching design, it becomes an important decorative feature for the façade.

0226 This exterior emergency staircase is truly unusual due to its two-way flights of steps: you may go in one direction towards one of the side entrances of the building, or take the other flight in the original direction, to keep going up.

0227 This apartment building has evidently limited space so the fire escape was built on the outside. Cantilevered platforms serve as landings and these are joined by spiral staircases.

0228 This original handrail has a remarkable undulating structure, resembling the waves of the ocean. These wave-like forms are interrupted by stainless steel studs. Installing the handrail was laborious, as it was located on a load bearing wall which was not parallel to the treads of the staircase.

0229 In this iron staircase, built by Lanbacher (Sonthofen, Germany), techniques have been used such as rivets, where the edges of different pieces are chamfered. These pieces have been built separately and assembled to obtain a complete system. The end of the staircase is supported by two big columns that feature eye-catching prints.

0230 Although they are inside a glass wall, these stairs are similar to those installed on the façades of buildings. Their design is the same as those of walkways which serves as a communal corridor connecting different dwellings, with a uniform and ordered layout.

0231 A central Art Nouveau-style wrought iron staircase was built in this house, built in 1916 and located in Colonia Roma, in Mexico City. This vertical entranceway allows access to six apartments located on two floors.

0232 The building is raised on posts over a dune overlooking the coast. Due to the house's elevated position, a wooden staircase with two sections and treads without risers was constructed.

0233 At the entrance area to this building – a 49 feet structure formed by metal and glass panels – a large staircase was built over the lockers. The washroom entrances are also located in this stairwell.

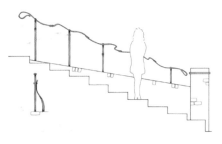

Staircase and handrail design drawing

0230

0231

0232

0233

0234 A cage of elegant vertical metal bars surrounds this staircase. Besides enclosing them, this structure serves to anchor the treads and support them, although this is barely visible from the outside.

0235 An internal, double-helix metal frame accentuates the design of this spiral staircase. The treads are paved in the same stone as the floor and have an integrated lighting system.

0236 The treads of this spiral staircase are anchored to a hidden metal frame, giving the appearance of a twisted backbone. The staircase features elegantly molded wood and a banister that seems to float in the air.

Staircase perspective view

0238

0240

0237 This Warsaw hotel lobby staircase hangs from thin steel cables, which support most of its weight. This anchoring system frees most of the steps from the need for supports, and allows a very large space to be left between the two levels it connects.

0238 These stairs connect two different levels sharing the same internal space of an airport terminal. They are lined with a structure consisting of a metal frame and glass sheets. This structure marks out the way for passengers and does not allow them to enter other areas of the site.

0239 In Google's amusing headquarters, the architects decided to adopt the playful spirit of the company and replaced one of the staircases with a metal slide, which not only has visual impact but also seems to have de-stressing effects.

0240 The wooden treads of this minimalist staircase seem to be held up by themselves on this concrete wall (they actually feature hidden internal metal anchoring systems). Similarly, the handrail appears to be attached on one end as if by magic – but that is just another optical illusion.

0241

0242

0243

0244

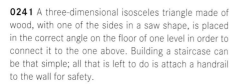

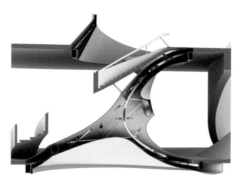

0241 A three-dimensional isosceles triangle made of wood, with one of the sides in a saw shape, is placed in the correct angle on the floor of one level in order to connect it to the one above. Building a staircase can be that simple; all that is left to do is attach a handrail to the wall for safety.

0242 A single ringlet-shaped length of metal outlines this spectacular spiral staircase, and serves as a handrail at the same time. The treads are joined to a simple upright post anchored to the floor and ceiling.

0243 Encased in a frame lined with aluminum panels, this staircase is all the more striking due to the contrast between the bright red interior and the metal outer skin. Its sinuous shape matches the curved lines of finishes and columns in the rest of the building.

0244 A plain banister consisting of two parallel metal bars traces the outline of this simple, minimalist staircase. The treads are lined in the same black flooring material, while the rest of the structure is painted black.

Three-dimensional section

0245 The seemingly raw, industrial finish of this staircase is a decorative feature in itself. The ends of metal beams piercing the wall become steps, with their upper surfaces faced with wooden panels to form treads.

0246 The original staircase in this clothing store is a combination of types. The first section is made of wooden blocks, a play on the shape of the display units, which are arranged in tiers. The second section is comprised of a simple metal frame with four steps.

0247 This series of plans are for the staircase in the atrium of the Nanotechnology Center of the University of Southampton in the United Kingdom. Designed as a sculptural inverted cone, the staircase has intermediate curved landings and is of an unusual thickness, required by fire safety regulations.

0246

0247

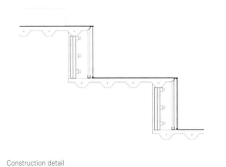

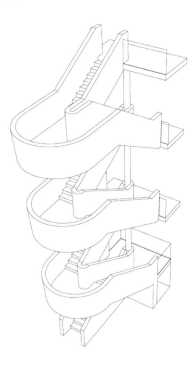

Construction detail

Three-dimensional section

0248 The interior of this residence designed by Emil Urbel features an original design solution to reduce the gradient of the staircase. The metal treads do not go right down to the floor; instead they connect with a somewhat wider wooden plinth that serves as the base.

0249 These wooden stairs, located in a private residence in Stockholm, Sweden, were created by the designers Gabriella Gustafson and Mattias Ståhlbom from the company TAF Arkitektkontor. The originality of this design lies in the angular arrangement of the treads.

0250 The staircase of this duplex is not only original in terms of the fixing of the steps to the wall, but also in the way it turns on a ninety degree angle, forming a small landing with a slightly wider platform, made of the same material.

0251 The two metal side guides of this staircase, or to be more precise, their winding shape, create the somewhat psychedelic layout of the treads. The staircase provides a very unconventional decorative element.

0252 The impressive design of this metallic cantilevered staircase tries to give the impression that the steps have been formed in the same way as you would fold a piece of paper. This design means that going from one floor to another is achieved via an element that hardly stands out as architecture.

0253 The elegant construction of this bannister, with frosted green-colored glass sheets crowned with a metal handrail, is a perfect marriage between the simple design of the two flights of freestanding concrete steps.

0248

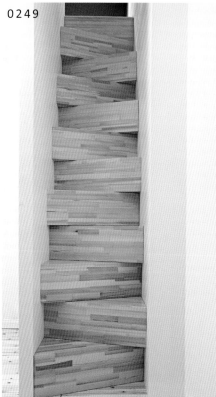

0249

0250

0251

252

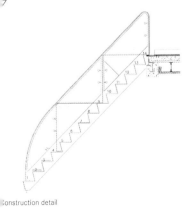

Construction detail

0253

0254

0255

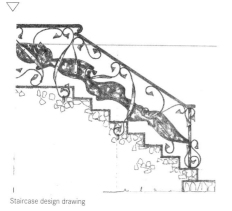

Staircase design drawing

0256

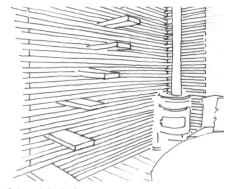

Staircase design drawing

0258

259

0254 The design of these entrance steps solves the problem of narrow spaces by fitting continuous mirrors on both sides of the steps, so that they appear to be triple the size.

0255 The process of creating a handrail starts with drawing a design, followed by constructing a model and finally, the process of creating it in wrought iron. Installing the handrail is the final step in the creation chain. In this case, the design is clearly modern and has a rusted look.

0256 When space is limited, it can be a good idea to install a staircase like the one in this image, with a light structure and small steps, yet surprisingly very rigid.

0257 In the Kobe House, the architect Hiroaki Ohtani used precast concrete slabs in a horizontal arrangement. This distribution allowed wooden stairs without risers to be inserted in the gaps between each slab.

0258 The design of this banister has horizontal glass panels to match the blinds on the nearby window. The practical architectural barriers then become a unifying feature for the interior.

0259 The stairwell of this penthouse is protected by simple metal banisters on three sides. To make this element less of a focal point, the wall side has no protection.

0260 A design like that of the elevator in this image is particularly recommendable for large spaces such as the entrance lobby of a hotel. For one or two floors, the housing is transparent glass, but upward from the floors with rooms, the elevator shaft is normal.

0261 Elevator interiors often suffer from poor lighting. Neon light fixtures inserted in the suspended ceiling help to overcome this problem and enhance the metallic finish of the interior lining.

0262 The granite covering the wall and framing the elevator door creates a striking contrast with the plain white panels lining the elevator cabin — a purposeful design strategy.

0263 One of the most in-demand models of door by the company Fermator is the two panel center parting glass door design, as used in the Palacio Juan Vareiola in Valencia.

0260

0261

0262

0263

Elevator plans, elevation and section

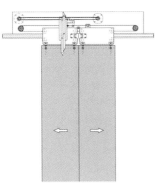

elevator door detail

0264 The Gran Mirilla model by Fermator can be installed either to modernize old elevators, or to replace them. In this residential building, a four-panel center parting door with printed finish has been used.

0265 This glass elevator was installed in the space created by the vertical transit staircase. As space was limited, a circular and transparent design was chosen, so as not to break up the visual field of the space.

0266 Fermator is a world leader in the manufacturing of elevator doors. In this case, for the National Art Museum of Catalonia (MNAC), an elevator was installed with the main feature of a two-panel telescopic door made entirely of glass.

0267 For the Fira de València, Thyssen Krupp Elevadores installed various Gran Mirilla elevators, with Fermator two-panel center parting doors. This project had a capacity of 12,000 people in its various rooms.

0268 Fermator offers circular models of cabins, thus creating adventurous, contemporary designs. At the Copenhagen Business School, circular doors were used for the two spectacular elevators.

0269 Elevators in public parking garages are essential for providing vertical access and communication. In the Puerto de Cambrils parking garage, an elevator with a three-panel telescopic door has been used, with a stainless steel finish.

0270 DomusLift is different from other models of IGV elevators because it can be installed in any space, from the smallest to the largest. It uses the Light-Touch, designed by Giugiaro, and classic models, combined with exclusive and elegant styles.

0271 The DomusLift Luxury Collection uses innovative materials and combines the most advanced IGV elevator technology with the characteristic style of Bisazza. This type of small elevator is ideal for installing in houses where the users are older or suffer some kind of disability.

0268

0269

▽

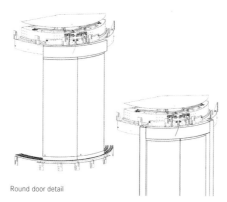
Round door detail

0270

0271

272

273

274

0275

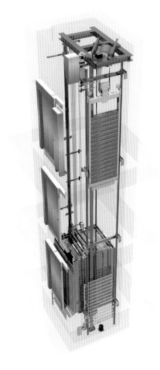

Axonometric projection

0272 The DomusLift-Small, which has reduced dimensions, is an elevator designed to facilitate movement between the various floors of public and private buildings. It is the ideal solution for older people, as it gives them independence and freedom from stairs.

0273 The panoramic cabins have an opaque rectangular part with vertical stainless steel panels, and a transparent circular part with safety glass and stainless steel profiles. The floor is paved with marble or granite and the ceiling is black and lit by spotlights.

0274 The main feature of Synergy elevators are the cabins, which are based on seven horizontal panels made from melamine, and also available in stainless steel or Formica. It is an innovative, functional and modern design.

0275 Latitude elevators do not have a machinery room and accept all kinds of rectangular shaped cabins, including panoramic. The machinery is located in the upper part of the elevator shaft and the operation closet is located next to the corridor entrance, preferably at the final stop.

0276

0277

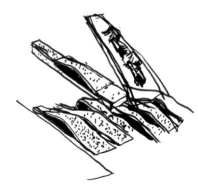

Sketch

Roof elevation and plan

0278

279

0280

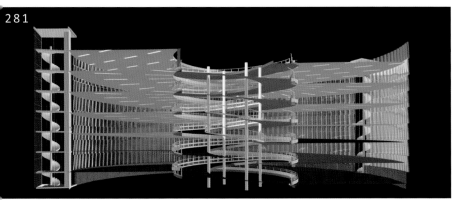

281

·282

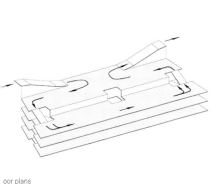

7

oor plans

0283

0276 The roof is constructed with an undulating metallic red grille, measuring 459 × 1,050 feet and occupying an area of 29,653 square feet. Entry to the structure is via a spiral ramp. This parking garage has 3,000 spaces for visitors to the commercial center.

0277 The roof of this parking garage is projected above the surface and becomes a pedestrian-only ramp, creating an identity for the square in which it is located. The interior is linked by ramps marking the path between the different levels of the parking garage.

0278 The most remarkable feature of this parking garage is its façade, which has sheets of stainless steel fixed to concrete columns using bands. This folded surface lets plenty of natural light inside.

0279 Located in the roof of an industrial hangar, this parking garage has a green-colored floor and circular plant pots, located in the garden to one side of the roof.

0280 In this parking garage, special emphasis has been placed on the signage. The different levels are distinguished by four main colors (red, yellow, green and blue) from the lights emitted by the polycarbonate tube lighting on the ceiling. Another element to help traffic is the border which marks out the parking area.

0281 The façade of this parking garage is made up of 800 glass panels, measuring 7.9 × 5.9 feet, placed on top of one another. These panels serve as semi-open windows which allow natural ventilation while protecting the cars from bad weather.

0282 The lighting used on the different levels acts as an intuitive resource for guiding the driver around the inside of this parking garage. All of the security and lighting equipment is integrated into beams and posts. The parking garage,which is oriented in a north-south direction, has access ramps set at right angles.

0283 The concrete finishes in this parking garage give the interior a rigid look, which combines well with the movement of the spiral. The circular floor, which raises up in seven turns of the spiral, allows natural light to enter through the open space.

0284 The interior of this parking garage was conventionally constructed with concrete walls; it is reached by two staircases located on both sides. These staircases are framed in a steel structure with a glass roof, which is a reinterpretation of the Cordoba mosque.

0285 The entrance to Biceberg is through a low-impact urban building which offers the possibility of installing various public services (interactive information, automatic sales, advertising) and extra services (bicycle repairs).

0286 The brightly colored façade transforms this normally boring space into an area whose graphic motifs really capture the visitors' attention. As well as being decorative, the icons of human and animal silhouettes guide drivers around the interior of the parking garage. The access stairs blend in with this graphic representation, with bright colors and words from the poem *Liberté* printed on the handrail.

0287 This parking garage has a central terrace with two emergency staircases at the sides. The central space increases ventilation and the entry of natural light. The concrete framework is oval shaped, allowing circulation in the center as well as parking spaces at both sides.

0288 The name of this commercial center, Europark, is lit up using luminous LED panels. Large serigraphic glass windows have also been used to increase the visual impact of the name. Next to the swimming pool, there are stairs leading down to the parking garage, which also directs users to the installations and children's play park in this area.

0289 The roof is raised up as an extension of the ground, creating an urban scene in the middle of natural surroundings. The roof folds of this parking garage are designed to blend in with the surrounding hills without detracting from the contemporary style of the structure.

0290 The ramp rotates on a circular axis, leaving an empty space in the center. Different points of lights have been installed to increase the impact of the majestic structure. At the sides there are columns which filter the light from the atrium inside.

0291 The pyramid structure of the twelve red skylights on the exterior of this parking garage is remarkable. These structures represent the only source of natural ventilation. Architects took inspiration from mosques to create these small architectural solutions.

0292 The black tiled floor is supported on columns of varying heights and at different angles created by the irregular slope. The interior of the basement is completely white and the columns are covered with a waterproof material to protect them during snowfall.

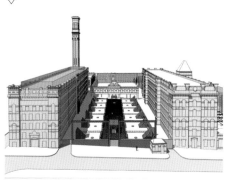

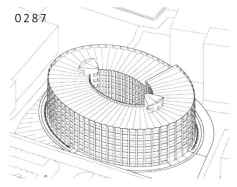

Perspective view

Perspective view

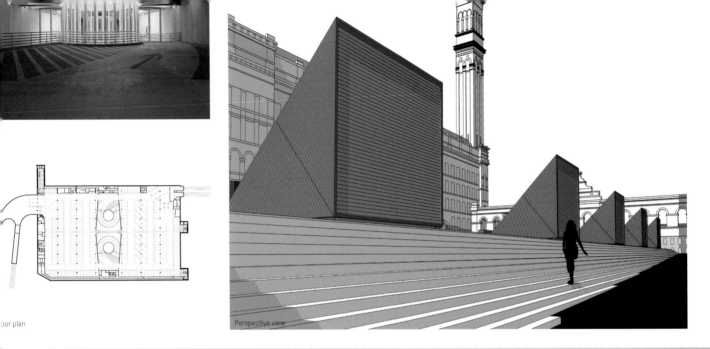

floor plan

Perspective view

292

0294

0295

Construction diagram

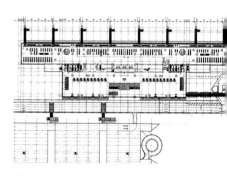

Floor plan

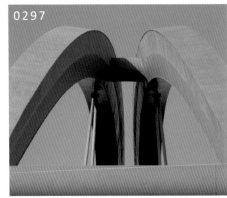

0293 Memorial Bridge is a thin L-shaped horizontal structure that crosses the Rijeka Canal. Steel is the main material used, forming part of the 154-foot length. The other materials used include aluminum and magnesium alloys and the large glazed balustrades.

0294 In highly populated cities, it is becoming increasingly common to connect buildings via raised walkways. In this case, a series of V-shaped pillars hold up the pedestrian bridge over a road.

0295 On walkways which serve as transit areas for passengers, a combination of glass in abundance and steel is used. These two materials impart a sense of lightness to the construction and a significant energy saving.

0296 The walkway connecting these two office blocks is covered with materials very similar to those used on the respective façades, although the metal border supporting it is more robust, as it has to support more weight.

0297 Although they meet at the top, the two arches crowning and supporting the weight of this bridge widen towards the bottom, to make space for the lanes of traffic below.

0298 The Copenhagen Opera House building features glass and marble bridges that connect to the auditorium, known as "the snail", which seems to float into the lobby. The exterior walls are clad with a warm wood treated in the same way as the wood of string instruments.

0299

0300

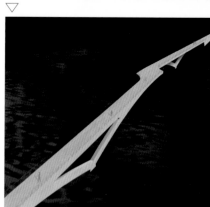

0301

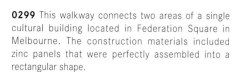

0302

Axonometric projections

0299 This walkway connects two areas of a single cultural building located in Federation Square in Melbourne. The construction materials included zinc panels that were perfectly assembled into a rectangular shape.

0300 The walkways of this bridge structure appear to be dislocated and are joined in a central stretch without pillars. This gives the impression that the two ends do not meet. During the night the balustrade is illuminated, creating a rainbow of colors.

0301 This architectural landscape is made up of walkways constructed in wood and located on the rooftop of an apartment block. In the plans, objects of daily use were installed such as tables and chairs for relaxing. In addition, original safety handrails were built.

0302 In the space between the bus station and where the suburban train passes, a walkway was built that serves as a link between the two. It is accessible for both passengers and residents of the urban area.

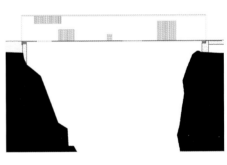

Section

0303 The construction of a new rail line adjacent to the freeway that leads to the national Reykjavik airport required a new system of routes and three pedestrian walkways. The design consists of a circular nucleus made from stainless steel and supported by large concrete columns. The columns and the roof are flexible enough to support thermal movements.

0304 Walkways and viewpoints connected to each other were built to form a panoramic path over the Gudbrandsjuvet waterfalls in Norway. Material such as white concrete and transparent glass has helped to create viewpoints with straight lines and sharp angles.

0305

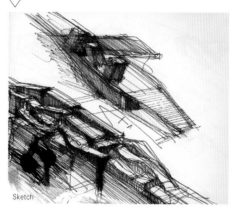
Sketch

0306

0305 On the lake situated in Parque de Beja, Portugal, there are walkways, pavilions and terraces that offer protection from the sun and invite relaxation. Concrete was used and it dominates the majority of the construction.

0306 In the main area of the Parque da Juventude, Brazil, there is an enclosing wall and the framework of buildings that are the remains of homes that were never completed. To make use of these remains, access was created by joining the enclosing wall with beams and metal pillars to the reinforced concrete on elevated walkways.

0307

0307 A wooden walkway connects the 20 natural swimming pools in the National Villarrica Park, Chile. This continuous ramp, without steps, marks the layout that permits the user to cover the entire ravine. The walkway stands out for its red wood and its straight and precise lines.

0308 In Stor-Elvdal, Norway, architects contructed a raised concrete platform measuring 69 × 79 feet that functions as a observation point that, at the same time, does not damage the natural environment and, prevents misuse by visitors.

0309 The gardening fair in Wernigerode, Germany, was the perfect occasion to create a modern park that connects the lakes in the area. The park is the backbone around a long central path called the "fish path", that is about 0.6 miles long. Materials such as wood, steel and cement have been used to build the path.

0308

Location and path plans

0310 In these Chilean hot springs a wooden walkway was installed that covers the course of the river and fits in perfectly with the natural environment. The platform was built higher than the ground in order to prevent visitors' damage the environment. The material chosen was wood that was dyed red but did not obscure the grain.

0309

0310

0311

0312

0313

0314

0311 The new DecorFlou collection features spectacular separation panels designed by Marc Krusin. This model by Omnidecor stands out for the lighting effects it projects into the spaces it separates.

0312 Japanese architecture has always paid special attention to elements separating one space from another. The wooden grid of the partition shown here ideal for only partial separation, is an example of the simplicity this company works with.

0313 With the Tree model, Omnidecor offer satin-finished glass separation panels with an attractive floral pattern. The frosted part filters the light while the part covered with the floral design allows light to pass without unfiltered.

0314 Bricks filled with different types of tinted stones offer an original alternative for separating spaces with surfaces that vary in opacity. These units, sold by Damglass, are hard-wearing and bring a casual and light feel to interiors.

0315 This unusual alternative was designed by the Arteks architects to set apart the fitting rooms in a clothing store. The logs are anchored to the floor and ceiling with metal fasteners and there is an inner curtain to cover gaps and protect the privacy of the space.

0316 A stairwell, which also acts as a storage space, is used to separate the kitchen area from the living area. The wooden stair covering provides a visual connection with the parquet floor of this private house.

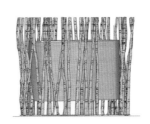

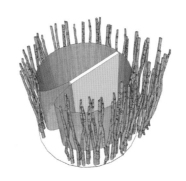

Plans

0316

0317 On one of the dividing walls between two rooms, a large shelf was built from small white boxes of varying shapes and sizes. This not only provides an area for storage, but lets in natural light.

0318 In this apartment, the kitchen, which on occasion doubles as a dining room, can be closed off at any time using the sliding doors. The kitchen was designed to allow access from several points and was built as a space partitioned from the most important area in the house – the living room.

0319 To separate areas inside this shipping company's building, Shwarz Design came to the conclusion that the best idea would be to install weathered steel wedges whose shape resembles the keel of a boat, an idea that gives the interior a lot of character.

0320 Folding walls were installed in this residence that serve either as space dividers or sliding doors, and that provide occupants with the privacy they need. These walls create compact volumes that can be used to isolate spaces.

0317

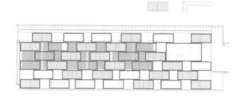

Book case side elevation

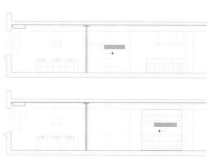

0318

Sections

0319

0320

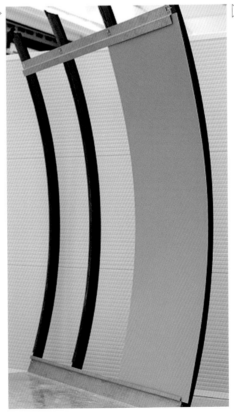

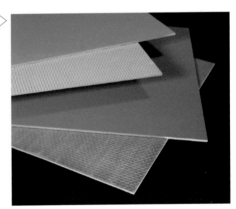

0321 A green brick wall that does not quite reach the ceiling acts as a divider between the kitchen and living room. It is designed as if it were a curtain concealing part of the kitchen. An opening was made in the center to make space for a long table that protrudes beyond the wall.

0322 Flexible fireproof ceramic panels by Saloni work perfectly with separations, sliding doors, and screens. Easily cut to measure for the space, they can also be covered, and come in a wide range of colors and shades.

0323

▽

Wall elevation

0325

▷

0324

▽

0323 The interiors of the Suntory Museum by Kengo Kuma give a clearly modern look to certain features of traditional Japanese architecture, as exemplified by the use of separators and wall coverings made from simple and unadorned wooden strips.

0324 The attractive tiger-print-effect flooring, present throughout the residence, is the main decorative element of these interiors, as it covers the floor, upper ramp, benches, table and the breakfast bar.

0325 While the walls of the rooms are covered with a continuous layer of wooden panels, transit areas use the same panels but unvarnished for a more rustic look. These are separated from each other by a few feet to enable air and light to pass.

0326 This wallpaper, named Chevron, is available in a design that is six inches in length, in various tones, and is particularly advisable for interiors requiring a certain amount of warmth.

0327 The two wings of this Kuala Lumpur residence are connected by a striking walkway built of nato wood. The banister was made by hand and installed on site.

0328 There are two patterns to the wood covering the walls of this computer room. One is comprised of horizontal strips while the other is of panels that alternate with different curves to create a relief with striking effect.

0329 Maya Romanoff created these wooden mosaics, which adhere well to all kinds of surfaces, and highlight the natural qualities of wood. The natural beauty of the patterns of the grain vary according to how the panels are cut.

0330 Horizontally overlapping and cut in such a way as to show their natural ruggedness, the strips of this flooring have been treated with a golden varnish, making them the perfect choice for environments requiring a certain intensity.

0331 This wallpaper, on the market under the name Coffers, is made from fragments of wood arranged in a parquet formation, which creates a feeling of depth and three-dimensionality. It is particularly good for covering ceilings, creating an especially dramatic effect.

0332 Available in tones ranging from very light to very dark, this material called Ajiro Diamonds can be applied in 2.8 or 5.9 inch pieces, depending on the specific visual weight desired from the diamond pattern.

0333 The seamless furniture and floor in this exhibition space was made using OSB (oriented strand board): panels of conglomerate woodchip board. This enabled the original floor of the space to be protected and lower production costs.

0334 The wooden strips used in this wall covering are cut by laser, and the inlaid work is done by hand by Maya Romanoff's craftsmen. Although it is costly, inlaid work is an extremely stylish way of increasing the elegance of your interiors.

0329

0330

0331

332

333

0334

0335 The wood lining practically all of the walls in this penthouse apartment features two very different finishes. The first is natural, polished wood running the length of the walls in the living space and concealing storage areas and the kitchen unit. The other, in electric blue, is reserved for the entrance area. The weathered effect of the wooden floor gives character to the interiors.

0336 The wooden mosaic tiles of this material look and behave exactly the same as ceramic tiles. The slight differences in tone bring intensity to the wall they cover.

0337 This wallpaper, sold under the name Ajiro, is so flexible that it can even be used in corners and around columns. It is the direction of the grain on each piece of the checkerboard that makes this such a spectacular design.

0338 The hardwood flooring of this remodeled house has dark tones that contrast with the colors of its grain. This produces an impression of relief and makes it a great decorative feature.

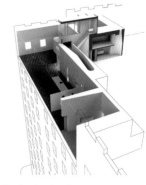

Perspective view of west section

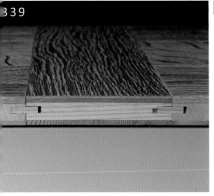

0339 This Schotten & Hansen parquet flooring has the advantage of being extremely flexible and can be made to adjust to different layouts. Furthermore, it can be cut on a curve without splintering.

0340 The interior design of this bar, by the Architecture Project, takes its inspiration from the classic overlapping of pallets in industrial warehouses. In this way, the spaces are defined by light structures based on strips of wood.

0341

0342

0341 The interior walls of this residence are almost totally covered in wide travertine marble tiles. This surface combines perfectly with the dark floors and ceilings and brings maximum brightness to the interior.

0342 The wall adjoining the dance floor in this night club is covered with an unusual layer of stone fragments that create a root-like pattern, matching the columns in the club.

0343 The limestone slabs lining one of the walls in this living area provide a warm, rustic touch to the interior spaces adjoining it, and echo the reception area flooring.

0344 The feature stone walls are combined with timeless materials such as wood, copper, and handmade glass. Large stone blocks become part of the furniture, serving as seats.

0345 The mammoth marble block comprising the island kitchen is the visual anchor of this residence. Marked with chalk by the architect at the quarry in Carrara, Italy, the block measures 21.3 feet in length by 3.3 feet in height.

0346 The interior wall of this bar in Brezno, Slovakia, has an original design featuring overlapping stone slabs. The largest stones are of a lighter color, and the spaces between them are filled with dark stones. A decorative motif is fitted into a octagonal space in the middle.

0347 The monumental aspect of the exterior of this new church is determined by the use of red brick. This type of stone has been used as a tribute to the industrial past of the area. In spite of the large dimensions of the building, it projects the necessary warmth for the interior of a church.

0348 When this Jewish temple was created, several types of stone were used for the finish. Different colors of marble were the most common material used in the paving and they add to the elegance and tranquility of the building.

0349 Blazed grissal granite from Spain has been used for the interior tiling of this meditation house. This type of material brings a sense of simplicity and somberness to the space, essential features in this type of construction.

0350 In the Islamic Forum built in the town of Penzberg, Germany, small stone slabs were used to cover the exterior. This type of material perfectly fits in with the cement and stainless steel used in the same building.

0351 The stone cladding, both in the interior and the exterior, is the main material used in this Catholic Church in Seveso, Italy. The design of this construction is committed to modernity; the characteristic shape of the stones reinforce the contemporary lines.

0352 By using marble, the architects have managed to create a calm space and a timeless design in the interior. These large marble panels, combined with transparent glass, make up this large architectural volume.

0353

0354

0355

0356

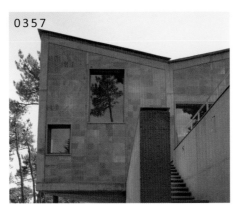

0357

0358

0353 The natural boundary of this park are the emblematic Harz Mountains, which inspire the different geological and mining themes that integrate into their design. An example of this is the limestone walls, which bring to mind the mining history of the region.

0354 In the reception of this Norwegian office building only stone has been used in the floors. For the construction, large local stones arranged irregularly were used. The architects used irregular forms to give it a more natural effect, just as they desired.

0355 Local stone is one of the most prominently used materials in the interior of this Australian home. On the walls, the large stones form a uniform mosaic while providing the interior with a rustic air.

0356 Cement and pebbles comprise the pavement that leads into to this Mexican home. The cement fixes the stones to the ground, so that they do not move and people can pass by without tripping or changing the pavement.

0357 The terraces of this home in El Escorial, Madrid, have become an extension of the home in the garden. This is achieved thanks to the outdoor paving stone that seems to continue on from the façades where slate has been used. The stones are arranged randomly and not in any order, creating an irregular mosaic.

0358 This original finish of a wall made from steel cages within which stones have been randomly positioned was the idea of the architect, as he wanted to use pure lines to show the construction process of a home.

0359

▽

0360

▷

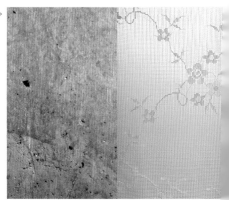

0361

▷

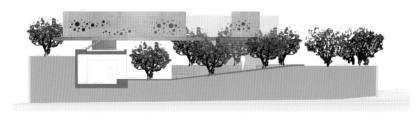

Section

South elevation

0363

0364

0365

ections

0359 This building consists of 24 10-foot-cubed cells that are aligned and stacked one on top of another, and is constructed by combining raw hard materials: stainless steel and concrete. The concrete walls with a classic unfinished look are a central feature.

0360 The most striking thing about this interior design project is not the relatively conventional use of concrete walls but rather their combination with embellishment, which gives them great character and makes them appropriate for offices.

0361 In this house – a modern interpretation of a typical Spanish country house – the architects placed special emphasis on integrating the house into the surrounding landscape. The gently undulating topography is reflected in the rising concrete ramps, and the holes in the exposed concrete walls are reminiscent of the ventilation holes in the tobacco drying sheds in the area.

0362 The original structure of this house has a design that looks as if it were a double staircase inserted into the landscape. The architects selected rough concrete as the principle material in the design.

0363 The spectacular nature of these interiors stems mostly from the way the floors organically merge with the walls and ceilings in a series of gentle curves. This detail is highlighted by making the concrete walls, covered only with a coat of paint, into the focal point.

0364 Concrete is a material that is very economical and it fits perfectly into natural settings. Moreover, its low maintenance costs and short construction times are key factors considered when choosing concrete as a construction material. The concrete has given this structure angularity of the outer shape and is also used in the interior.

0365 The architectural structure of this building is fabricated from reinforced concrete. The descending ramps that surround the central atrium and elevators are also built using this material, which gives the structure an elegant and minimalist style.

0366

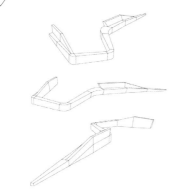

0367

Three-dimensional representation of the concrete built elements

0368

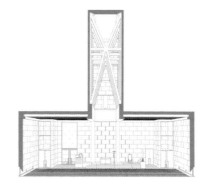

Section perspective

0369

0366 In Mount Street Parkland, in the Australian city of Melbourne, a small open space was created that serves as a passageway for passengers and a place to rest for the city's inhabitants. The result is a long, winding construction, made from cement, where an illuminated panel made from diodes is installed that displays text messages on the screen.

0367 Large concrete slabs were used to create an inviting and open space to the faithful in this Japanese Baptist Church. The reddish tones can be seen in the interior ceiling and walls. This material adds a minimalist touch to the design.

0368 The structure of this church is mainly made from reinforced concrete and fitted with wooden slats. On the roof of the main building an oblong volume has been installed, with large windows that allow natural light to pass to the interior.

0369 Several concrete slabs have been used for the main entrance of this Islamic temple that is made up of two large structures. They simulate open doors that welcome believers with inscriptions in Arabic and German.

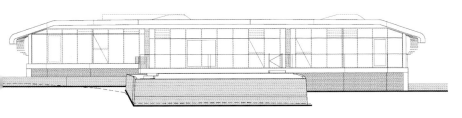

vation

0370 Curved cement beams also serve as handrails on this observation point platform. The floor is also made from concrete and has rectangular openings covered with glass that let the natural light pass through to the terrain below.

0371 Due to topographical demands, this building was constructed from reinforced concrete. This allows minimalist patios to be created with scarce vegetation. In the entrance, concrete panels have been used to create a cantilevered structure, forming a small porch.

0372 Both the structure and the roof of this home have been made from concrete painted white. On one of the side façade, the roof is elongated to form a large terrace paved with merbau wood. This type of cement absorbs the suffocating heat typical of Australia.

0373

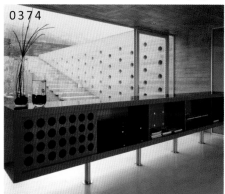

0374

0375

0376

0373 The separations between the different existing spaces on the lower floor of this beachside home were built using reinforced concrete. In this case, a wall has been built to separate the kitchen and dining room and an opening has been made to visually connect the two spaces.

0374 The architects designed a house without a façade so that it could act as an observation point for the nearby valley. As the budget was limited and the size of the home could not exceed 1,500 square feet, cement was the most suitable material to achieve the desired results.

0375 Concrete was used as the most ideal material to build a partly-buried home. The underground corridors are built with concrete walls and roofs. In this way, the home remains cool all year round, in addition to transmitting an austere image.

0376 In this home located in Turkey, concrete was used to cover the walls and pave the floors. The architects used this material given that the owners wanted a low cost and austere look inside the house.

0377 The inside of this North American home has been designed in continuous, elegant and clutter-free spaces. The white-painted concrete has given rise to said spaces, lending it the feeling of a loft. The industrial-style details and materials reinforce this image.

0378 Generally, there are no partitions in the interior of this Peruvian home. The only exception is the kitchen in exposed concrete, where there is an opening that serves as a bar. The concrete complements the terrazo, which is used as flooring in the majority of the spaces.

0379

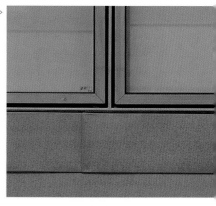

▷

▷

0380

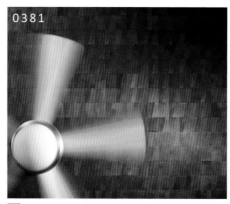

0381

▽

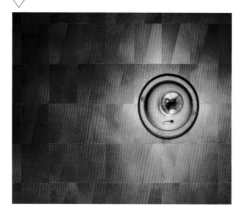

0382

0379 This streetcar stop, created for the Hannover Expo 2000, has an attractive copper covering, with the usual turquoise patina that this material acquires. The panels are different widths, forming an original assembly pattern.

0380 The semi-exterior areas of this remodeled Portuguese farmhouse were faced with artificially-rusted iron sheets, a finish that combines perfectly with the stone walls, the only remnant of the original structure.

0381 Maya Romanoff recently presented an innovation in wallpaper, offering rolls of real copper in squares or trapezoidal shapes measuring 11.8 × 11.8 inches, lined in polyester for easier hanging.

0382 Available in 2.8 and 5.9 inch pieces, this synthetic wallpaper imitates the shine of aluminum, but is much easier to clean and install. Its commercial name is Basketweave.

0383 On the second floor of the EVO restaurant, located in Barcelona, the Bouquet bar offers panoramic views of the surroundings. These open and close to suit the clients' wishes. In this space there is a foyer and a lounge room where cocktails are prepared. The floor, the ceiling and the decoration of the columns are metal.

0384 Stainless steel was used both in the accessories and equipment utilized in the restoration of this kitchen. Each element has been placed with care, so that it forms part of the overall design of this kitchen, while maintaining a close relationship with the other spaces.

384

0385

0387

0386

0385 The handrails, made from parallel metallic tubes, bring out the curvilinear and winding forms of this pathway. This material creates light and organic forms that perfectly integrate with the natural location where they are installed.

0386 A copper metallic finish is used in the decor of to give it an original and majestic look. Rectilinear strips follow the line established by the different modules and counters located on the lower floor of the building.

0387 Metal sheets were the solution to finish off the different façades of this home. Corrugated metal sheets that extend over the north façade and even cover the windows were used. In front of these sheets the same micro-perforated material is used.

0388 Aluminum runner blinds have been used for the entire façade of this apartment complex, like small mobile pieces of a puzzle. This material gives the building of 230 homes a Soviet air, where the main concern is to make the most of the floors to create different sizes and distributions of apartments.

0389 The complexity in the design of this restaurant located on the roof of the Esperia Tower hotel stems from the creation of the large dome with steel and glass framework. This original oval dome sitting 344 feet high allows guests to enjoy a fantastic view of the city center of Barcelona.

0390 On the main façade of this botanical garden, weathered steel was used in combination with exposed concrete. These materials were already present and the architect wanted to recover them in the creation this botanical institute in order to maintain conceptual continuity.

0391

0391 Iron was the main material used in the construction of the International Conventional Center in Barcelona. On the outside, it has been used as an expansive and majestic metal structure. Inside, there is a large room with a metal roof.

0392 On the interior façade of this student residence, zinc has been used as a metal finish. In addition to zinc, black bricks, wood and exposed brickwork have been used. This chromatic evolution imparts a vitality to the character of the university center.

0393 The concrete façade of this hotel was painted blue and orange, combined with aluminum and glass panels. This metal finish gives it a majestic air, as well as integrating it with the metal walkway that joins the two towers.

0394 This home is built on a solid metal structure, which allows the house to totally integrate with nature and at the same time it protects it from adverse climate conditions. For the exterior, galvanized steel sheets were used.

0395 The metal pergola is one of the most attractive elements of this Japanese home. The light that falls through the pergola creates an attractive shadow effect. The use of these modern materials projects a clear and airy image of the buildings.

0396 In this project, steel, the most widely used alloy in the world, is used to create an elegant staircase. The combination of this metal with glass creates a vertical area of circulation that climbs a concrete wall and connects an open living room on the lower floor with the individual rooms on the upper floor.

0392

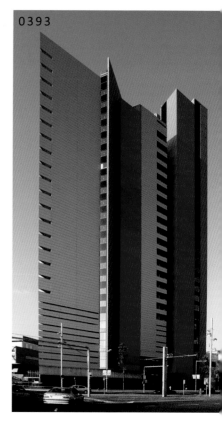

0393

394

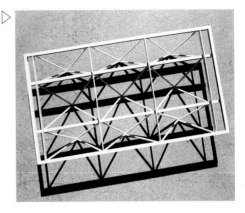

▷

0395

396

0397

0398

0399

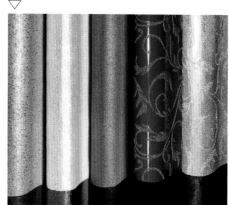

0400

401

402

0397 In addition to providing a punch of color, the padded polyurethane and imitation leather panels used in this loft apartment serve a threefold function: a door to the children's bedroom, a covering for a hidden shelving unit, and acoustic insulation for the living area.

0398 The panel covering the back wall of the new performing arts theater in Graz, Austria, is a decorative feature. A series of violet plastic molded arabesque shapes were assembled on site to create a strikingly visual pattern to match the color of the seats.

0399 Beadazzled, a glass-encrusted wallpaper, is the first of its kind. The synthetic material it is made from is one of the most hard-wearing and flexible options for covering walls, and comes in different patterns.

0400 Artigo designs and manufactures high-performance rubber floors. In this case, the Kayar model is built with coconut fiber and rubber — organic materials that convey an idea of contemporary nature.

0401 Sold in 17.7 × 17.7 inch pieces, this wallpaper by Maya Romanoff is available in geometric shapes and floral designs. It is particularly good for covering large areas due to its large size.

0402 The Komodo range of vinyl wallpapers is available in different pastel shades, and is now being sold in panels measuring 54 inches in width. Its design attempts to imitate the shine of a lizard's skin.

0403 The texture of the rubber flooring is directly inspired by the grain in wood. Here the design has been interpreted so far as to become abstract, natural and pre-geometric. This original material is characterized by the tactile surface created with irregular grain of varying thickness and depth.

0404 Mold technology is the crux of the Zero.4. flooring. This method allows a seemingly random distribution of circles with different diameters, generated through a geometric progression calculation.

0405 A large blue polyurethane wave welcomes children to this pediatric dentistry practice, and turns the frightening experience of visiting the dentist into a fun and exciting experience. Modern and casual, the impact of the design comes from its sinuous shapes and bright colors.

0406 Sold under the name Vinyluse, these plastic adhesives are an economical and very individual way of decorating interiors. The designs are of floral motifs and cartoon characters and are available in different colors.

0403

0404

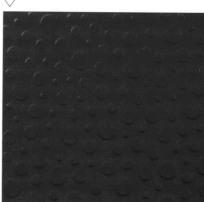

0405

0406

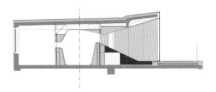

Section

0407 The hallway of this modern public building features a wall built using individual plastic slats with LED backlighting in many colors to create a futuristic and truly striking ambience.

0408 According to the architects, this is a "dune-shaped interior landscaping" project. To achieve these walls, four elements were used: clear polyurethane, elastomer paint, stamping of anamorphotic images, and a coat of clear protecting varnish.

0409

kitchen island

This is a new project to take into account a new dimension of kitchen. It is a new way of conceiving the worktop, derived from the modular project, and supporting in a vertical and horizontal direction. A panel that provides the possibility to realize your own kitchen, the "tablemade" way. An effect, so to say, can comprise the modular and functional workings that to ends up to create the most effective and efficient cooking.

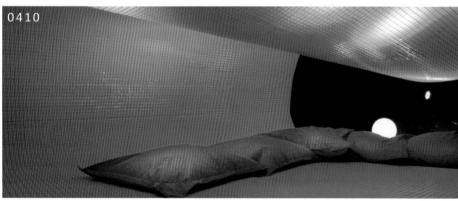

0410

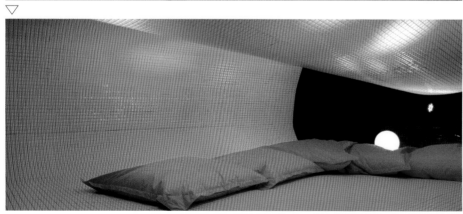

0411

0409 The Lammax ceramic panels by Saloni are highly recommendable as an option for wall coverings in areas like kitchens, or as countertops or stair treads. Available in a wide variety of colors, they are fireproof and insulate beautifully.

0410 The aim of this exhibition project was to give a certain feeling of movement to a wall covered with ceramic glazed tiles. To achieve this, the tiles have been fixed to a curved mesh, which in this case serves as a wall.

0411 Travertino-Lavico (Arkim) is a versatile tile that brings together concepts and technologies. This porcelain is unalterable, long-lasting and hard-wearing. The deep red color has a great natural expressive force with a shiny polished finish.

0412 Imitating nature can sometimes create unexpected design effects. In this case, the use of porcelain creates a glossy and modern effect on the surface. The Gugong model by Arkim reproduces the appearance of tree bark and the linear characteristics that show the age of vegetation.

0413 Porcelain tiles give surfaces a dynamic three-dimensional appearance. Floral and geometric patterns, as well as "crocodile skin" textures are designs that are characteristic of the FINN model (Arkim), providing a tactile feel of leather.

0414 Aparici is a Spanish company that produces ceramic and porcelain finishes. The photograph shows Carnival ceramic tiles arranged on the bathroom wall. The covering is warm and suitable for this kind of space.

0415 The rectangular panels that cover this façade are a revolutionary product, a 0.1-inch-thick porcelain ceramic sheet measuring 3.3 × 9.8 feet. Its resistance is greater than that of granite and it is lighter than aluminum. These panels adapt to all types of surfaces and can easily replace tiles and glass.

0416 The material used for the Helsinki airport floor is white Life measuring 31.5 × 31.5 inches. This is full body technical porcelain. This type of porcelain is most commonly used in public spaces owing to both its extraordinary resistance and its large format.

0417 Ceramic tiles have been used in the bathroom of this office building. The color, format and texture make them an attractive element for the floor. Ceramic is long-lasting, non-slippery and easy to clean.

0418 In this family home located in Sant Cugat, Spain, Vivendi has been used as the main material in the architecture. This material is full body technical porcelain, which allows for the creation of a ventilated façade through the mechanization of the rear piece.

0419 A sauna was installed in the basement of this home. A running door separates it from the rest of the spaces. The division is formed by small ceramic tiles that form floral figures. In this space, ceramic has been chosen because it improves thermal features.

0420 Here, the floor and the walls of the bathroom have been covered in ceramic mosaic tile. This material is used in particular for floors because it is anti-slip and offers simple solutions for these types of spaces.

0421 Once mosaic tiles have been installed, they do not require any maintenance apart from normal cleaning. In this case, they have been applied to kitchen walls for their durability, and resistance to biological and chemical agents.

0422 In the southern area of this home, a wall with small red ceramic tiles is prominent. This wall leads from the exterior, where the pool is, and connects the hall to the living room, where it delineates the dining room.

0423 The architect, landscaper and owner wanted to achieve an interaction between the home and nature. In order to do so, they agreed that the home would maintain continuity with the crystal blue water in the pool. To emphasize this effect, different colored porcelain mosaic tiles were used.

0424 An ivory and dark blue marble finish on the mosaic tiles, along with glass and ceramic have been used in the paving of the floor of this pool. In addition to the decorative aspect, these materials were chosen for their low-cost maintenance.

0425 Ceramic is the most common material in this project. Its use provides a sense of elegance and sobriety to the overall project. The white-yellow combination in the paving of the pool is also reproduced in the adjacent circular arbor.

0426 The landscape architects used blue ceramic marcite tiles to create original designs both on the bottom of the pool and on the walls that make up the fountains. To emphasize this effect a combination of different blue tones were used.

0427 These interiors designed by Splitterwerk combine surfaces faced with medium-density fiberboard panels with others covered in a metallic gold paint normally used in the auto industry, to which AutoCAD-designed, cut-out adornments have been applied.

0428 Dubbed "Colors Square," this urban landscape project is an example of how differently colored pavement can be used to define spaces and achieve a cheerful atmosphere, in this case adapted to the characteristics of typical users.

0429 Most of the interior spaces in the André Malraux Library, designed by Ibos & Vitart, feature bright red, a color present in the synthetic flooring of some areas and columns and walls, and in many pieces of furniture. This kind of color scheme is highly recommendable to provide a corporate identity to public institutions.

0430 Modernization of this Stockholm apartment simply involved changing the wooden floor; the originality with which the colors were enlivened turned this remodel into a unique and very economical design.

0431 The small space encouraged the designer to conceive of a simple and economic way of defining spaces. The solution was a drastic change in the color scheme of walls, from neutral white to bright red.

0432 Technicolor-inspired surfaces and stripes of color are used in this young editor's apartment. All the colors used were painted on a narrow section of wall next to the front door. The corridor was painted with random stripes of vibrant color.

0433 In this house, a bright range of cinematic colors has been used. The green-yellow and glossy gray-magenta separate the kitchen from the living-dining area. The colors intermingle: the dining room color invades the kitchen area and vice versa, to achieve harmony between the spaces.

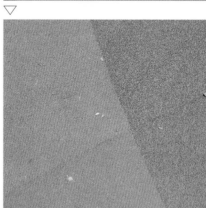

0430

0431

0432

0433

0434

Design drawing

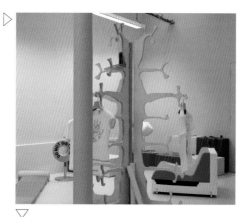

0435

0436

Side elevations

0437

0438

0434 This store, founded by four independent creators, is a shopping platform that collectively sells, furniture, CDs, clothes, shoes, etc. Matali Crasset and Marie-Anne Dudouit designed this common space that makes reference to several meanings. The harmony of the ensemble is highlighted by the baby blue color that is combined with the wide chromatic range of the furniture.

0435 L'Annexe du BHV is a new space designed by Matali Crasset for the BHV Belle Épine store. Some 31,200 square feet has been dedicated to young people who come together to practice leisure activities, take part in workshops and exchange ideas. For this reason, electric and acidic colors have been selected and used to define different spaces.

0436 The remodeling of an old kindergarten provides a new interactive and communicative space in the interior as well as a multifunctional façade. The design for Taka-Taka-Land was based on the book by the same title by Astrid Lindgren. Lime green and lemon yellow are the colors that stand out on this façade built using recycled materials.

0437 The design of this Ricoh office is made from compact units that include meeting areas, smoking areas, office areas, etc. The colors define and delimit spaces to create a pleasant work atmosphere.

0438 The Werd restaurant and bar stands out for its original bright green painted floor and its large spiral staircase in bright red. These two colors contrast and combine together in harmony in the entire interior design. Other complementary colors in the design are black, ochre and opaque white that emphasize this chromatic harmony.

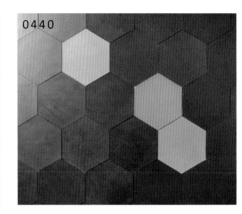

0439 In this recreation center, the architects placed special emphasis on pleasing graphic elements that accompany the user. Pastel tones are used to emphasize natural light entering these spaces, which provides dynamism and clarity to the sporting pavilion.

0440 These original tiles are surprising owing to the material they are made from: leather. The hexagons can be used to cover both floors and walls and they can also be adapted to the shapes of a handrail or a worktop. They are available in different colors and are fitted according to the owner's taste.

0441 This restaurant in the Reina Sofía Museum, managed by Sergi Arola, presents a contemporary design, which was created by Jean Nouvel, where metal and plastic predominate. The reddish toned colors emphasize the light, creating a spectacular dining space in all senses.

0442 The restructuring of the F.C. Barcelona gym and changing room is a modern and comfortable space, adapted to the needs of the first-class team. Sound-proof walls were installed with glass doors and an indirect lighting system. The corporate colors (blue and deep red) completed the end design.

0443 Intense red gives spaces such as a corridors, dining rooms or lounges a vibrant energy. Sometimes it is used to create visual points of interest, as in this staircase, where the color emphasizes access to the second floor.

0444

PORTA INTERNA A TIRARE
INTERNAL SWING PULL

PORTA INTERNA A SPINGERE
INTERNAL DOOR PUSH

RIVESTIMENTO
COVER

PORTA INGRESSO BLINDATA
SECURITY ENTRANCE DOOR

0444 With this innovative design, Domina combines various types of interior doors into one single model and offers an elegant way of making the door in the same wood as the paneling on the wall where it is to be installed.

0445 Covering a door with the same wallpaper as on the adjoining wall is an eye-catching concept for maximalist interiors where the intention is to convey a feeling of continuity.

0445

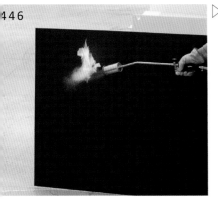

446

0447

448

449

0446 Lammax porcelain cladding panels designed by Saloni offer an elegant alternative for door facings. They also provide fireproofing for interiors where they are installed.

0447 When there is no passageway, doorways connecting rooms should have as wide an opening as possible to guarantee the entry of abundant light. For spaces of this width, doors with fixed or folding panels are a smart option.

0448 The glossy metal finish on this door not only offers fireproofing but also conveys a sense of elegance and luxury to interiors. The brocade-like triangular pattern makes it special.

0449 When the door and the surrounding wall are covered in the same material, the continuity has a tremendously warm effect. In this case, the wood's original color has been left unchanged to enhance the contours.

0450 Acid-etched glass doors are perfect for separating spaces and guaranteeing privacy without blocking light from entering. The finish can also include decorative patterns.

0451 This door opens in a truly inviting way, which alleviates the awkwardness of it having to occupy the entire width of the passageway. Two-thirds of the wooden panel opens while the remaining one third is fixed, and both are of the same material as the surrounding walls.

0452 Despite remodeling this country house, the architects wanted the new doors to evoke tradition. They were given an old look with metal studs, diagonal grooves, and barred windows.

0453 W_Concept is a new project designed by Silvelox to provide two entrances to the same building — one for vehicles and the other for people — combined on the same uniform wall. These doors can also be installed individually and come in five different wood finishes.

0454 The Wayl model, designed for Domina, has a strikingly-designed metal door frame. This is a soft frame incorporating an aluminum panel that slightly separates the door from the wall it closes on.

0455 This door, covered in the same light veneer as that used on the walkway floor, has two small rectangular openings and an elliptical shape at the top offering a note of color.

0456 The silver finish of this door perfectly matches the colors of the interior walls and floor of the space it was chosen for. A vertical band marks the area of the door handle while the rest of the door is covered with horizontal bands.

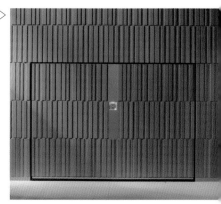

0454

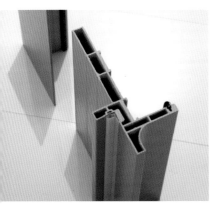

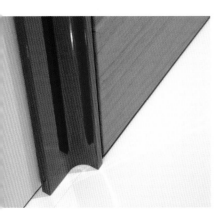

0455

0456

0457

0458

0459

0460

0461

0457 It is becoming more common to see doors faced with two different colored woods, almost always in bands. The result is an extraordinarily modern piece that can be matched to the same tones used in the interiors.

0458 The design of this door makes use of the space where the two panels join to break up the expanse of the wooden surface with a decorative symmetrical motif: two triangular openings let light through and surround the area of the door handle.

0459 Placing a porthole in a door not only connects the spaces separated by the door, it is also an elegant decorative feature with a strong nautical feel.

0460 Few materials are as versatile, economical, resistant and long-lasting as PVC. This image shows a colorful example of the possibilities offered by this material, becoming more popular in use in doors and windows.

0461 A simple door with pale blue acid-etched glass separates the living area from the hallway in this apartment. This material guarantees privacy in the space but also ensures that natural light can enter.

0462 This aluminum door, with its large and striking curved handle, perfectly blends in with the metal blinds that cover its glass panes.

0463 This metal security door frame not only makes the door resistant to break-ins, but also helps to highlight the wood of the door, increasing its beauty.

0464 The doors of this office play with the wooden strip motif decorating the corridor walls. A series of lines formed by metal threads runs horizontally over them to lengthen the line of the wall.

0465 A door can become the focal point of a room. In this case, a striking naïf-style floral print not only decorates the surface of the door panel, it also covers the frame.

0466 This interior door, with its elegant checkerboard pattern of openings formed by a wooden framework, features an oriental feel that is at the same time traditional and cutting edge.

0467 What is really attractive and original about the design of this door is that the wooden frame does not appear to surround the acid-etched glass pane on all four sides, but only on the two vertical sides (the frame at the top remains hidden behind the door frame).

0468 This interior door handle features a design that is simple and slender. The collar surrounding the handle is smaller so as to cover less of the wood.

0469 Instead of hinges, the central panel of the door separating the living area from the reception area in this home has center pivots. In this way it opens like a revolving door, but acts like a screen when ajar.

0470

Door design drawing

0471

0472

0473

474

Door design drawing

0470 The front door to this building is based on spirals of various sizes and in different positions, as seen in the craftman's design drawing. The structure makes use of plant-based designs and straight shapes, making it both elegant and original.

0471 The Fiori door, designed by the Italian craftsmen Seno & Siffredi/Colpi di Martello, shows the harmonious combination of different materials, such as wrought iron and copper. There is a growing demand for creations of this kind, meaning that craftsmen have had to become innovative.

0472 The front entrance to the Riscal cocktail bar, designed by Tino & Ricardo Barbosa/Barbosa Space Projects, is an example of how interior designers are now integrating design and architecture, with the use of traditional wrought iron as a decorative feature.

0473 The front entrance to this building was created in keeping with the architecture of the dwelling, in an elegant and romantic style, thanks to its decorative spirals. Before projects are approved, the craftsmen creates either freehand drawings or AutoCAD simulations; both options enable the client to approve the project.

0474 There is a long tradition of decorating front doors to buildings, as it represents the entrance into the private domain. Although the final product sometimes differs from the original sketch, classic designs such as spirals always prevail.

0475 The simplicity of the basic structure of this exterior door made of wood and wrought iron contrasts the wrought iron work on the handle and railing. The malleability of wrought iron enables the creation of spectacular designs that really showcase the craftsmanship, which is reflected in the marks left by the strike of the hammer.

0476 The Leaf door, almost 6.6 feet in height, is made from tempered steel. It is decorated with floral motifs, which show the originality of the English craftsmen at Bethan Griffiths/Artistic Ironwork.

475

0476

0477 The intricate design of the front door of this chalet transforms it into a decorative element of the highest degree. When it is open, the metal leaf overlays the metallic wallpaper on the wall inside, resulting in an attractive overlapping effect.

0478 The unusual design of this door — two panels of the same size divided into 12 horizontal bands — seems more appropriate for a closet than an exterior, an idea reinforced by the handles that take the the form of small knobs.

0479 The revolving door giving employees access to this office building is unusual in the way its mechanical workings are completely exposed through the total transparency of the glass. The circumference of its frame is entirely in view.

0480 An increasingly popular technique is replacing wood with aluminum or steel, while maintaining the designs where wood tends to be used, as in this panelled door. Until recently, these metals could not be molded in certain ways, or the processes involved were very costly.

0477

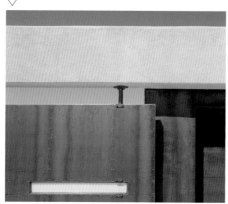

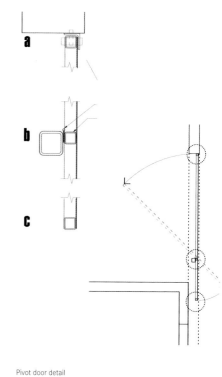

a

b

c

Pivot door detail

0478

0479

0480

0482

483

0484

0481 This door is made from panels of wrought iron, 0.2-inch-thick, intersected with oak panels. The houses' front doors were created in iron with the idea of creating a feeling of security.

0482 A simple triangular-shaped cut drawn on the façade over the plans allowed the emergency exit to be created for this building. The simplicity of this solution is the key to its striking design.

0483 This restaurant door has a clearly retro style, very reminiscent of the 1950s and very popular in a number of US cities like Miami. A spectacular effect is created through the combination of wood with a semi-circular glass inset.

0484 Doors with sophisticated woodwork continue to be worth taking into account when decorating a façade. Geometric patterns and metal studs are some of the most common features.

0485

0486

0487

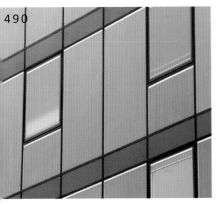

0485 Combining modernity with tradition, glass blocks were used to act as a screen to provide privacy from the street and to surround the terrace, which connects the kitchen to the interior. This original structure protects privacy and provides the interior with more natural light.

0486 Clear glass windows from ceiling to floor allow abundant natural light to enter. Individual roller curtains have been fitted on each window to adapt to different needs. On the exterior, the existing façade combines glass with wood finishes.

0487 The vaulted glass panels of these elliptical structures are strikingly flexible. These windows are adapted to the framework of the structure and make this bubble-like building possible.

0488 The particular feature of these windows lies in the possibility of sliding them vertically to guarantee good ventilation. The angled windows enable the window sill to be suitably widened.

0489 The unusual way the window frames are inserted into the façade of this building are a modern take on traditional construction of this architectural element, with a rectangle of wood holding glass panes. In this case, the frames seem to have been pushed into the wall under pressure.

0490 The attractive façade of this office building features a series of folding hatches, which when closed fit tightly to the building without adding surface relief.

0491 Lemonpack is a patented product that uses glass bricks as a container. They are a modular and decorative element that works perfectly as a separator between spaces, giving the wall a three-dimensional feel.

0492 The expanse of glass covering the façade was installed using an innovative steel structure and a concrete support, which acted as a support point and tensioner. The metal frame was created in collaboration with local manufacturers.

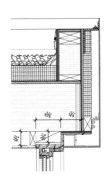

Window header and cantilevered roof section

0493 This simple streetcar stop shows an extremely ingenious way of providing support and tension for the sheets of glass on its base. A few simple plastic ropes are stretched between some knobs on the base, ensuring perfect elasticity.

0494 The new CriSamar® STEP range by Sevasa offers eight designs of anti-slip glass designed specifically for corridors, staircases, walkways, ramps, decking and roofs you can walk on, both indoors and outdoors.

0495 Skylights are large openings in the ceiling that allow direct sunlight or changing light to enter depending on the time of day. Glass floors on bridges increase the natural light on the lower floors of the building.

0496 The architects decided that each of the four buildings that make up the Musée du Quai Branly should have a different façade. The main construction is a walkway in the form of an enormous curved glass wall supported by pillars.

0497 Glass dominates the main façade of this residence. Large windows were constructed to allow the owners to enjoy the views of the sea, and to be able to see the interior from outdoors.

0498 On the roof of this building, which is used for teaching music, openings have been created as skylights. These structures made of translucent glass allow natural light to enter, creating a well-lit environment, which is beneficial to the work being carried out in these music rooms.

0499 The exterior aspect of the façade of the National Air and Space Museum's Steven F. Udvar-Hazy Center is perfectly smooth, and in some areas has straight and rectangular-shaped glass windows. This saves a considerable amount of energy, as the building enjoys natural light for most of the day.

0500 The original façade of the extension to the Denver Art Museum, which resembles Japanese origami, features various polygonal elements at right angles, made from granite, titanium and glass. Inside, these right-angle glass openings create a spectacular display of light and shadows on the floor.

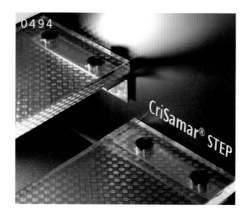

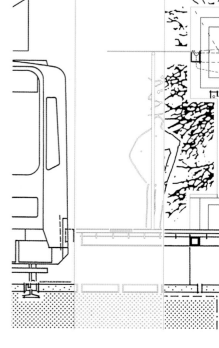

Platform section

498

499

0500

0 5 0 1

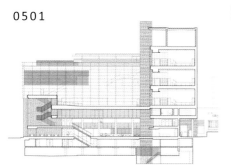

Section

0502

0503

0501 The extension to the Canadian School of Ballet was planned as a vertical campus entirely made up of transparent sections. Large rectangular, vertical were installed both inside and outside windows in order to let sunlight enter and to be able to see what is going on inside the different spaces.

0502 Glass panel walls amplify the space in the entrance lobby and maximize the amount of daylight that enters the building through its main entranceway.

0503 One part of the façade of this home is entirely made of glass in order to allow natural light into the home and create a sense of space. Glass is used in the windows and walls as well as to separate spaces. The house opens onto a patio located on the lower level that is safeguarded by a matt glass wall.

0504 Glass is the main feature of the architectural complex The Quartier Concordia that brings together engineering, art and business faculties. This material has been used as a handrail for the staircase and in large windows on the façade and in the central atrium.

0505 The clear and intense light of the Danish coast inspired the design: to make three of the façades and the roof of the home out of glass. There is a copper covering that coats the walls and the roof. This material creates giant horizontal windows.

0506 The design of the façade of this mall, located in Zurich, had to be in keeping with its strategic location in the city's busiest district. The glazing in the façade allows onlookers to watch the daily events inside.

0504

7

Side elevation

0505

0506

Side elevation

Section

0507 The large central skylight of the Guggenheim Museum in New York is an example of architectural virtuosity. An organic ring of six arches support the glass roof.

0508 This circular skylight spans the meeting point of this hotel lobby. The matching rug marks the lighted space as a rest area. A series of recessed halogen spotlights around it serve the same purpose at nighttime.

0509 The completely transparent roof of this area turns it into a semi-exterior space. The skylight is built like a gabled roof, with a triangular frame of metal beams forming trusses to provide internal support.

0510 The foyer of this convention center benefits from having a completely transparent roof. The glass sheets are sloped like a gabled roof, with the special feature of having certain sections where the gradient of the structure changes at different heights, which makes the roof narrower.

0511 This glass roof is held up by the tension of the arch composed of tubular steel supports. Rather than a grid, the pattern formed by the frame resembles an uneven row of bricks.

0512 The roof of this shopping center consists of a vaulted structure formed by square glass panels framed by a metal grid; some of the panels are in two layers. The same structure incorporates the lighting system rails.

0513 An acid-etched skylight is a recommendable solution to offer good lighting to interior spaces that are distant from light entering through windows. The skylight of this residence, positioned at the apex of the gabled roof, fulfills this function perfectly.

0514

0515

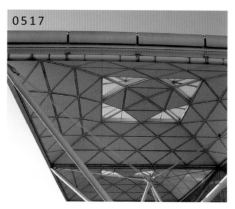

0517

0516

0518

0514 A simple rectangle perforating the suspended ceiling and separated from the outside by nothing but a panel of clear PVC may be the solution to problems with interior lighting. The penetration of light from above creates dramatic effects, like theater spotlights.

0515 This large pyramid-shaped skylight combines blue acid-etched glass with clear glass. The latter is only used in the triangular panels along the vertices, preventing excess light from entering.

0516 Large semi-circular skylights are becoming increasingly common in the design of public buildings. Many of them incorporate an automated cleaning system that works like a windshield wiper turning the entire width of the structure.

0517 The modern canopies in front of the arrivals hall of this airport feature a clever system to prevent excessive shade. Some of their component triangular panels have been replaced with clear plastic, which allow more light to pass through.

0518 This simple skylight hatch comprised of laminated glass panes features a tilt and turn opening and closing system. Pushing the crossbar opens the hatch and provides ventilation for the interior spaces under it.

0520

0519 This expanse of skylights features the ability to open one of the panels to enable air to enter through the space in the open hatch.

0520 The elegance and the polished finish of the metal frame supporting this skylight turn it into a distinct decorative feature. The complex structure of straight beams and arches is architecturally striking.

0521 These two sophisticated skylights in a gabled roof not only change their slant by means of a central pivot, but also offer users the possibility of lowering or removing blinds that attach to them.

0521

0522 The barrel vault of this building was sheathed in white acid-etched glass panels to enable plenty of light to pass through without compromising privacy in the interior spaces.

0523 This type of vertical skylight, more akin to a hatch, is often used in high rise buildings and office buildings where the façades are simple glazed grids. Normally one or two panels are installed as hatches to allow proper ventilation of the interior.

0524 The skeleton of this structure imitates traditional architectural forms using modern materials. The light metal frame supports glass sheets in an arrangement once done with materials like wood in a typical gabled roof.

0525 The increasingly fashionable design for footbridges and pedestrian transit areas is to cover them with vaulted skylights, which prevents them from becoming claustrophobic tunnels.

0526 This boldly visual vaulted roof is extraordinary as a result of the grid of metal nerves that sprout from each arch, and for the abundance of vertical supports that create the arcade.

0527 The impressive dome of the British Museum in London spans the pre-existing buildings like a secondary and artificial atmosphere. A classic skeleton of triangular fractals supports the enormous glass hemisphere.

0528 The frame of this dome features the typical design of a vault forming a hemisphere, except that in this case it is crowned by a sizeable hole that connects to a large central support pillar.

0529 The large skylight spanning this atrium is held up by a unique system of tubular supports. It is striking how the tensioners on the frame create downward arches in a curve contrary to that created by the roof.

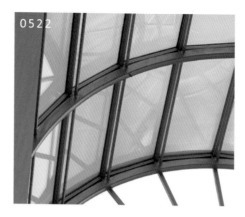

528

529

0530 The large octagonal skylight over this atrium determines the layout of the interior, as the overhanging balconies from the different levels trace the same shape.

0531 The skylight of this atrium features a very unusual design: its relief traces the outline of the same angular pattern on the glass walls of the building, this time horizontally instead of vertically.

0532 The glass vault spanning one of the lobbies in this hotel has been decorated with nautical motifs. This cheerful and simple design in stained glass is an updated version of one of the most traditional features of religious architecture.

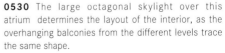

0533 The glass roof of this shopping mall mimics the split levels of the interior it spans – it rises in steps – with a large vertical panel halfway up.

0534 The impeccable façade of this building features a transition between the completely vertical wall and the vaulted skylights over the cantilever marked by lights. The glass panels of the façade are all of the same size.

0535 The support systems for the roofs of a number of public buildings are becoming more complex. In this case, a series of diagonal tensioners that create pyramid-shaped structures hold up the wide expanse of this glass roof.

0536 The tinted glass panels are adapted to this roof by a simple system of tubular guides placed in succession like the slats on the base of a bed. The visual effect is stunning.

0537 The stairwell of this residential building is spanned along its length by a broad skylight made of wide glass panels, barely broken by the fine lines of the metal frame holding it up.

0538 The lines of skylights on this public building create spectacularly organic shapes. They are positioned in intersecting planes, in an almost expressionist style, in the design of the roofs of this complex.

0539 The atrium of this shopping mall is illuminated by a large skylight with the same vaulted design as the roof of the building, which spans the wide void left between the metal beams of the structure.

0540 Skylights can often help to create amazing visual effects. In this case, the grid design completes a three-dimensional cube perspective when added to the grid formed by the different interior levels of the complex.

0541 In some cases, the size of a glass vault is so expansive that the design needs to incorporate one or two staircases so that the top can be reached without difficulty in order to facilitate cleaning and access for maintenance workers.

0542 The skylights over this semi-exterior space that crowns the transit areas of a hotel are held up by a simple system of circular fasteners that are becoming very fashionable. These fasteners combine strength with discretion as they barely interrupt the transparency of the glass.

0543 The roof of this building is supported by a complex mesh of triangular tensioners. The shape of the large skylight bringing light into the area imitates the design of this support structure, adding coherence to the project.

0544 The series of skylights in Melbourne's airport terminal show how these lighting features can also be decorative. In this case, the circular holes are inside square voids in the suspended ceiling, creating a unique play on geometry.

0545 The spectacular design of this skylight features a metal frame resembling the whimsical shapes of snowflakes arranged in fractals. This is a spectacular decorative effect.

0543

0544

0545

0546 A very common design for industrial buildings and large structures such as airport terminals or train stations, is to open a central area in the roof for a skylight, which is particularly suitable when the distance between the middle of the building and the windows is very large.

0547 Given the variety of sizes they come in, and the fact that they are often made from synthetic, highly-resistant material, bubble-shaped skylights are a recommendable choice for allowing light into interior spaces like parking garages and shopping malls.

0548 The design of this hotel room is striking for the abundance of windows and skylights. It was convenient to perforate the roof for several skylights to guarantee good lighting, since it overlooks a narrow and dark street.

547

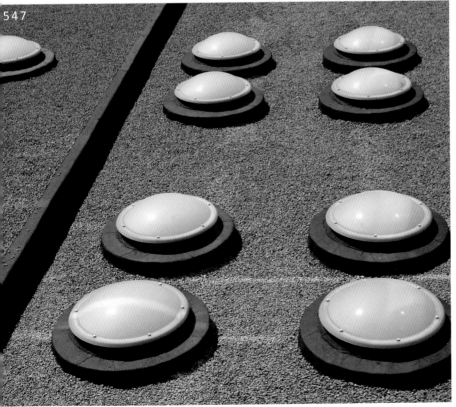

0548

0549 The large skylight spanning this atrium is so similar in design to the façade that it seems as if somebody has placed a mirror between the two. This design adds unity to the project, in addition to a sense of continuity.

0550 This elegant skylight crowns the corner of a foyer in a pentagonal office building. The metal frame gives it height and traces a pyramid shape that gives a greater sense of space to the interior.

0551 On occasion, glass panels can be used as canopies, rather than as parts of the roof as skylights. They can cover porches or terraces and protect them from rain without preventing light from reaching these spaces.

0552 The design of this expansive glass roof focuses more on the support structure than the light that enters. Normally such a large number of beams and crossbeams would not be necessary, but here, visually breaking the transparency of the skylight is an architectural design feature.

0553 A design solution often employed in public buildings and shopping centers to guarantee proper lighting of interiors is a large skylight spanning the area of the stairwell. In this way, light can also reach the lower levels.

0554 Opening a skylight in the roof of a building not only allows light to bathe the interior, but it also makes the space immediately below suitable for vegetation.

0549

0550

0551

0552

0555

0556

0557

0558

0560

0555 Sunlight was very important to the architects of this building. For this reason, 50% of the south façade is glass, a proportion that reaches 100% on the north side. The canopy-like skylights installed on the outer layers allow light to enter at a greater angle.

0556 The vertical panels of synthetic material that connect the balcony railings with the roof act as blinds to limit the incidence of solar radiation on the façade. Their bright colors also offset the color scheme of the rest of the façade.

0557 The exterior of this house designed by Axel Nieberg is embellished with the use of acid-etched glass slats. They are arranged vertically on the lower level and horizontally on the upper to protect the privacy of the bedrooms.

0558 This building by Tillner & Willinger features a complex protection system formed by curvilinear metal slats, necessary to keep interior spaces free from excess sunlight, given its location. The panels were designed to coincide with the height of greatest solar incidence on each window.

0559 This country house by Tham & Videgård Hansson Arkitekter features windows in both the walls and gabled roof. Folding brise-soleil shutters installed on the windows provide protection from two different angles of sunlight penetration.

0560 To avoid letting in excess heat and light, the façade of this villa designed by Paul de Ruiter features a system of sunblinds comprised of 10 horizontal panels in western red cedar wood that fold up or down depending on the weather.

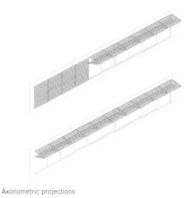

Axonometric projections

0561 This attractive residence by Paul de Ruiter features an elegant system of camouflaged folding sunblinds. As they are made using the same vertical wooden strips as the rest of the façade, they blend into it without interruption when lowered.

0562 For the façade of this social housing complex, an economical solution that goes back to one of the oldest architectural traditions in the world was applied. The retractable sunblinds have an outer layer of bamboo latticework, a material that always functions perfectly to filter light and keep interiors cool.

0563 With a modern and functional appearance, Venetian blinds fit well in spaces with clean and simple lines. They can be also placed between the two panes of glass in double-glazed windows in order to protect them from dirt.

0564 The huge vertical sheets on this building help to separate the frontal spaces corresponding to each of the apartments, and also transform the façade into a distinctive element.

Façade construction details

0565 The use of large windows in the majority of the walls of this coastal house helped minimize the building's visual impact on the environment. In addition to its use in the windows, glass was used as a protective balustrade on the terrace.

0566 The adjustable Lamistar blinds, by Griesser, have a clear aim: to optimize the amount of natural light to the interior work spaces. The slats are located in the lower area and unfold upwards, so that the user can direct, close or open the slats at any location.

0567 The need to retain a slope at the entrance was the inspiration for creating this curved gate. As primary function of the gate was to block off the path rather than for security, the designer could play with the different elements.

0568 These railings are from the grounds of a parish church in Canale, Italy. The geometric patterns intermingle with flowers, so that both are combined at various points. The winding forms are a clear example of the spectacular designs that can be created thanks to the malleability of wrought iron.

0569 This spectacular gate and garden entrance to a private property was created in wrought iron by the craftsman Miquel Xirau (Vilanova del Vallès, Spain). This kind of construction has always been important in the architectural design of any dwelling: it serves as a screen uniting private and public spaces.

0570 Small spheres were used to join the bars that make up the final structure. These have a double function: as joints and as decoration. The simple decoration of the vertical poles alternates with the rounded joints.

0567

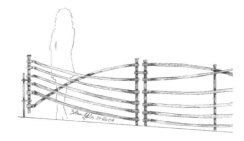

Enclosure design drawing

0568

0569

0570

Front door design drawing

0571

nt door design drawing

0572

573

0574

0571 Spirals, rolls, scrolls and floral decorations feature in the design of the German firm Fibo Leuchten-Schmiedeeisen. The joints are electrically soldered, and then they are held in a vice and beaten. The demand for wrought iron-look pieces has increased in recent years.

0572 This rural house's front door and gate were constructed by the Italian firm Seno & Siffredi/Colpi di Martello. This modern gate is made of vertical bars with scrolls meeting at the top and in the middle.

0573 In this entrance and gate to a private house, Catalan artist Miquel Xirau has created some elaborate, innovative and surprising designs. The workmanship reflected in the design defies the presumed rigidity of a material like iron.

0574 Railings and gates have always symbolized the marking out of private territory; the entrance represents access to a sacred area. This is the case with this Gladwyne front door, created by Ricardo Cabrera/Artesano Iron Works, which is the entrance to a private property.

0575 The primary functions of doors and entry gates – protection and access – are softened by the use of delicate and stylized decorative elements, such as scrolls and whorls. This door was expertly created by the craftsman Miquel Xirau.

0576 The entrance doors and gates of this project are made from sheet metal painted white and decorated with wrought iron. The design, inspired by nature and with zoomorphic and floral motifs, is very common in this kind of artisan work.

0577 Santi Fuchs is an artist and craftsman who works with iron. His original creations are based on his own unusual style. The iron is subjected to high temperatures which enable it to be easily manipulated to resemble electrical cable.

0578 The gates to this house, with an apparently simple design, feature a representation of a fisherman's net. The knots and joints, which resemble real rope are represented in an extraordinary way.

0579 Two materials have been used to make this door to a private house: copper and wrought iron. Eight copper panels are joined together in an iron structure. The central and side joints feature roses as a remarkable decorative element.

0580 These original gates are made from panels of weathered steel. The characteristic rusted finish has been widely used in contemporary urban sculptures and is now become popular for private designs.

0581 The use of scrolls with an elegant finish with plant designs is a feature of the work of craftsman Miquel Xirau. His work also features a remarkable three-dimensional aspect: the strokes of the hammer can be seen in all of the decorative elements.

0582 The malleability of wrought iron means that at high temperatures, the materials can be twisted, folded, joined or assembled. Closed or open curls and loops are the most common curved shapes created by craftsmen.

581

0582

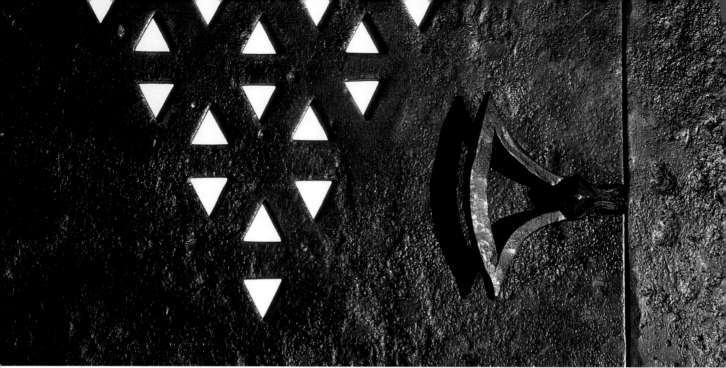

0584

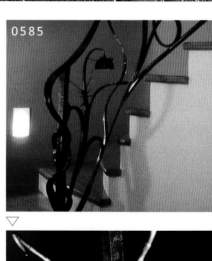

0585

0586

Door design drawing

0583 In some interiors, the fireplace becomes a main feature: that is why spectacular designs are being created for grates. In this piece, the characteristic feature of the wrought iron finish can clearly be appreciated. Triangular and square shapes dominate the design.

0584 This staircase and handrail in wrought iron were made by Scarsi Bernardo for a wine producer. The design is characterized by its sculptural realism, which reproduces the vines exactly, according to the wishes of the client, who wanted a design linked with the grapevines.

0585 The general demand by clients for architectural details constructed in wrought iron is based on models from past eras, but with staircases and handrails, original and almost sculptural forms can be created.

0586 In this photograph, the use of the curved wrought iron can be seen: possible when an incandescent temperature of 1292–1652°F (700-900°C) is reached. The iron is bent over an anvil by striking it with a hammer until the curvature and desired radius is achieved.

0587 The front entrance to the workshop of craftsman Scarsi Bernardo, in Canale, Italy. In wrought iron manufacturing, different finishes are created to give the metal a certain look. In this case, an ochre-colored finish has been used.

0588 The Liberty door is an elegant design by Scarsi Bernardo (Canale, Italy). Made from wrought iron and wood, the only decorative detail is in the center, with a representation of floral motifs and fruit finished in green paint.

0589 The use of wrought iron structures in architecture means that architectural elements seem lighter and more ephemeral. Wrought iron has enabled detailed design and decorative elements to appear in the front railings of private residences.

0590 One part of creating wrought iron is the cutting, which involves partially cutting the iron so as to be able to go on forging it. The designs and shapes involve many cuts being made in the same material, as in this case, where the wrought iron hinges require this treatment.

0591 Wrought iron craftsmen have done their most detailed, refined, ornate and individual work on elements such as locks, keyholes, latches or door handles. This is a classic door handle designed by Forjas Artísticas El Francés, Spain.

0592 Over the last decade, the use of wrought iron in architecture, as in this door handle at the entrance to a shop, has increased considerably. This has prompted a return to artisan work which is highly valued by the clients, who are buying exclusive pieces.

0593 This spectacular and original front entrance to a winery was designed by Miquel Xirau (Spain). The chosen decorative theme is the vine. In this door, the characteristic marks in the wrought iron can be perfectly appreciated.

0594 This wrought iron doorknocker was constructed and designed by Forjas Artísticas El Francés, Spain. This firm, with a long family tradition in wrought iron art, creates exclusive, individually hand-made pieces, which makes each product unique.

0589

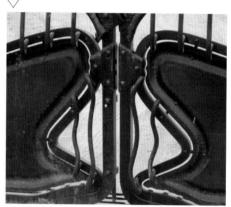

0590

0591

0592

0593

0594

0595 This image shows the hard work that the team of Italian craftsmen at Scarsi Bernardo puts in to creating wrought iron structures. The winding, sculptural shapes of these structures convay a lightness which seems imposible due to the heavy look of the iron.

0596 The malleability of wrought iron enables the creation of spectacular and original designs, like this one for example, formed of interwoven winding iron pipes, as well as others imitating a mesh or net. It is a clear example of the way in which architecture sometimes blends with sculpture.

0597 This handrail for a private residence is constructed in medium carbon steel. The design of this banister is based on a Louis XVI-style French palace, with floral motifs wrought and embossed on a 0.1-inch-thick sheet of steel.

0598 In this monumental handrail constructed using a combination of brass and wrought iron, the joints look like circular springs surrounding the shapes that resemble tree roots.

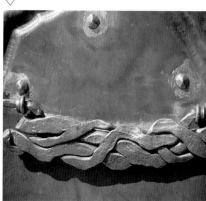

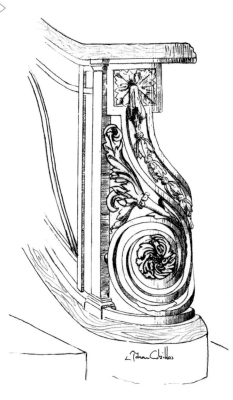

Handrail design drawings

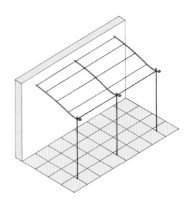

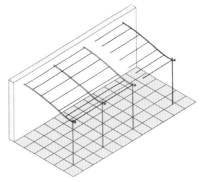

Pergola design drawings

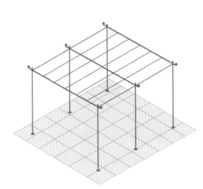

Pergola design drawing

0599 This Solaire pergola is a versatile structure that can be assembled without the need for screws. It adapts perfectly to the measurements of the intended location and can be formed of two, three or more units depending on the needs of the client.

0600 The Italian firm Unopiù offers various models of wrought iron pergolas. These kinds of structures can be circular, square or octagonal and located in private or public gardens. In this case, it is a self-supporting flat roofed structure.

0601

0602

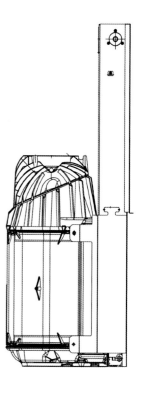

Section

0603

0601 Most glass fireplaces are usually gas-fired. The designs are created using translucent glass so as not to obscure general visibility within the space, since many modern fireplaces are installed in the center of rooms.

0602 This model is one of the first large scale built-in designs. Its main features are the double combustion system – the option of drawing in combustion airflow and convection flows of air directly from outside – the special aeration system and the wrought iron structure.

0603 This innovative rectangular wall-mounted fireplace is sold by Gaya. Its appeal lies in the fact that the flame appears to emerge from an opening at the front, like from the mouth of a spring.

0604 The impressive minimalist design of this fireplace could not be simpler: the cement floor leaves space for a metal hearth area, while the flue is hidden behind the projection of the wall, at the height of the gap which runs along its width.

0605 Bloch is a French company well-known for commercializing contemporary designs for custom-made fireplaces. This is a model of a wood-fired weathered steel chimney. Its design is in keeping with the rustic feel of the house.

0606 This fireplace, manufactured by Dovre, can be easily converted into a corner hearth. This is achieved using a conversion kit that is comprised of a panel of wrought iron and two pieces of vermiculite.

0607 Mixed design fireplaces (metal and glass) are usually installed in the center of living areas. For the most part, they are located in the place where the central table would be. This original design takes its inspiration from bonfires that are burned in the countryside.

0608 The Hwam model is a minimalist wood-burning stove. The large curved glass screen and elegant design let you see the flames burning. It has a sliding door system to make handling easier.

0609 Despite the size of the glass, this fireplace can be opened from the top with one single movement. This elegant design is easy to use and very practical, and its wide width enables it to hold large pieces of wood inside.

0610 The Stûv 16 is an original design of fireplace that can be fitted without major work into an existing gap or into a new chimney so that the user can enjoy efficient additional heating.

0611 This version of the Hwam model has an extraction system for ash. Ash is extracted into a container and aspirated through a special filter. In this way, dust created by the ashes does not spread throughout the house.

0612 Uni Flame is a contemporary fireplace designed for both outdoor and indoor use. It has a light look and standard measurements: 38 × 16 × 18 inches. It uses bio ethanol, a sustainable energy fuel.

0609

0610

0611

0612

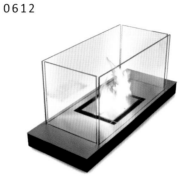

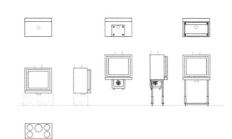

Dimension drawings

0613 To cover up a space in a wall where a chimney or opening used to be, the Rais Insert is an elegant solution for any open fireplace.

0614 The Audrie model, with a rustic and traditional look, is constructed using Nayont Fine stone that has a standard circumference of 7.9 inches. There are other versions of this kind of fireplace, made with French patina and antique stone.

0615 Stûv 16-cube is a wood-burning stove that is mounted on a plinth so that the majority of the heat diffuses out through its walls. The hearth is equipped to extract the air that it requires for combustion from outside, therefore not disturbing the circulation of air in the house.

0616 This fireplace has a simple design, where the only thing you can see between the fire and the masonry is a 1.5-inch metal frame. For the creators of this model, Gérard Pitance & Antoine Offergeld, their priority was being able to see the flames and the architecture.

0617 In these types of fireplaces the door opens to the front to make cleaning the inside of the glass easier. They also have low environmental impact and high performance. There are different models which vary in width, from 17 to 53 inches.

0618 In this fireplace, the interior glass disappears, and in this way allows the flames to be seen without obstruction. The use of partially raised glass prevents high pressure in the event that the flue is insufficient, and allows the hearth to be integrated into a low, horizontal space.

0619 This cylindrical stove has three doors that rotate around the combustion chamber, in such a way that the mode of operation can be changed by hand, quickly and easily, with one simple movement. The glazed door provides a good view of the flames, in total safety.

0620 Installing the Stûv 30-in model is very simple if there is already a space for it to fit into: there is no need for pipes, air outlet grilles or electrical connections, provided that the hearth easily fits into the chimney breast. Nor is there any need for finishes or decorative work.

0621 This original electric fireplace can be mounted on a wall. It is a closed hearth that is as powerful as the best wood-fired stoves. It recharges at night and burns steadily, even after many hours.

0622 The T-EYE is a stove with a very original and futuristic design. Its special shape with rounded contours ensures that it will fit easily into any required space. As the hearth rotates, the heat can be directed according to the users' requirements.

0623 The T-LOFT model has an elegant design and functional options. It has a glass door so that the combustion inside the hearth can be seen. This model is extremely flexible in terms of its placement.

0624 Chimeneas TNC offers a wide range of hearths resembling traditional heating methods and creating a warm atmosphere in a home, without overheating the surroundings. These units can be incorporated into any interior decoration scheme and have no visible brand name on them.

0617

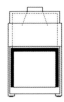

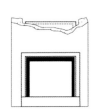

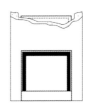

Dimension drawings

0618

0619

0620

0621

mension drawings

0622

mension drawings

0623

0624

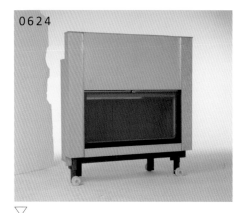

0625

0626

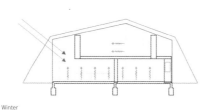

0627

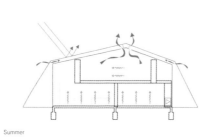

Winter

Summer

Bioclimatic diagrams

0628

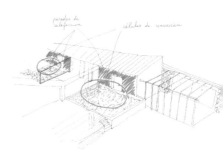

Convection heating scheme

computer generated drawing of a soft skin dwelling

0630

0625 These prefabricated flooring and roof panels come fully incorporated with radiant floor heating, hot and cold water and waste water pipes, ventilation and electrical systems.

0626 The heating system in the floor and walls is formed of polyester tubes integrated into the hangar enclosure, which heat the interior space much quicker than other systems. Using stainless steel for the enclosure enables the foundations to be lighter and lower impact.

0627 Passive climate control systems, based on creating microclimates between the layers, are reinforced by active strategies such as concrete radiant floor heating powered by a gas furnace, and a hot/cold pump for summer.

0628 Water acts as a true bioclimatic catalyst in this residence. The two fountains — north and south of the main porch — encourage the circulation of air by convection, in order to expel heat in the summer and collect it during the winter.

0629 A green roof always provides thermal benefits for heating the house and keeping its inhabitants warm. In this house, built mainly from concrete and glass, the use of a roof of this type is justified by the high thermal inertia of a material such as concrete.

0630 This Texas property is thermally insulated using 9.8-inch polystyrene panels placed between two layers of plywood. The façade, which is almost completely glazed, has a coarse-grained opacity to block out sunlight and prevent overheating in the interior spaces during the summer months.

0631 Construction based on layers of materials, including those which generate microclimates depending on the time of year, is an example of energy efficiency over the useful lifespan of this dwelling. The outermost layer has a solar protection filter, which reflects 50 to 75% of solar radiation.

0632 The Davies Alpine House greenhouse for Alpine plants required a bioclimatic design in order to conserve the species it houses. The definitive volume has a shape that fans out like a peacock's tail and contains a labyrinth-shaped concrete base underground. Its ducts cool interior air inside during the day and create cross-ventilation.

0633 Rostock University library is located at the entrance of the new university campus. The technical concept used, called *bauteilaktivierung*, consists of water pipes inset in the concrete foundations, which are connected to geothermal sources and thermally regulate the building.

0634 This sculptural building with a 29.5 × 29.5-foot floor plan has a gabion façade formed by 365 baskets that contain around 40,000 stones, weighing a total of 28 tons. This façade bioclimatically regulates the house all year round.

0635 This office building consists of three glass prisms, separated by segments and attached to a large glazed roof. Side openings in the central prism allow cross-ventilation. The garden in the lobby also creates natural air conditioning in the building.

0632

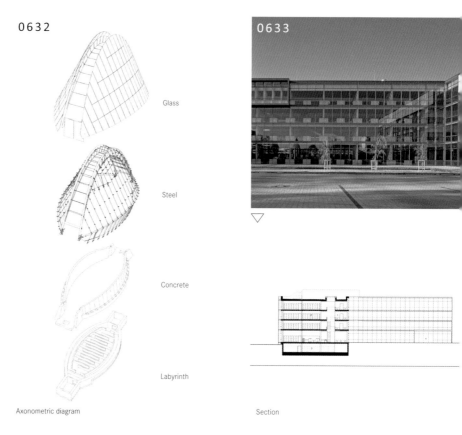

Glass

Steel

Concrete

Labyrinth

Axonometric diagram

0633

Section

0634

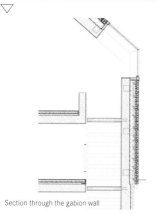

Section through the gabion wall

0635

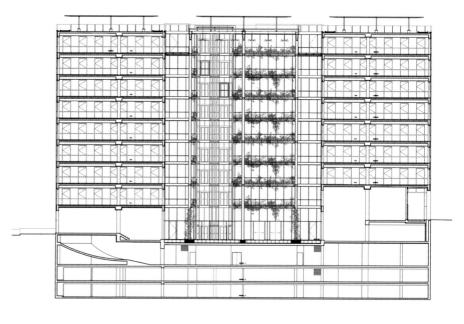

Longitudinal section

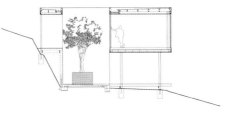

Cross section

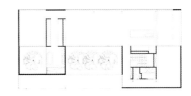

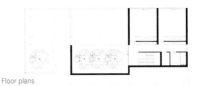

Floor plans

0638

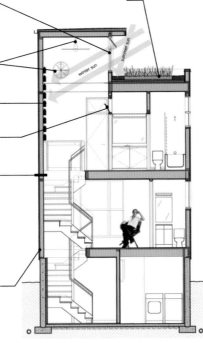

Cross section

0636 This property is a lightweight construction consisting of a prism broken by wooded courtyards that cool the air running through the interior spaces. These courtyards create cross-ventilation, which together with the thermal mass of the concrete slab of the living room, results in a natural air conditioning system.

0637 The Dome spaces fulfill geo-biological requirements and are free from electromagnetic currents and water. The building rotates and in winter is heated by solar orientation techniques. In the center, a fireplace provides supplementary heating.

0638 The F10 house is thermally regulated by its green roof, which is an excellent insulator. During the winter months, the sun enters through the clerestory window and hits a wall of bottles, which acts as a heat sink.

0639 The ethylene tetrafluoroethylene membranes of the Beijing Olympic pool, also known as "the water cube", allow high levels of natural heat radiation in the building and pool. Since the pool is heated passively and not with heat pumps, this entails a 30% reduction in energy expenditure.

0640 In this laboratory building, the depth of each balcony varies in alignment with the cardinal points. In this way, the designers can exactly control the shade that is generated in each part of the building, which drastically reduces the cooling system expenses.

0641 The Sea Ranch, in California, has two natural air conditioning strategies: first a green roof with a skylight that filters the sunlight, and, second the glass deck in the outer end of the living room, which functions as a solar collector during winter.

0642 The front façade of this home faces a lake, which allows for the cross ventilation that is produced by air currents generated over a layer of water. This passive strategy permits the acclimatization of the house in the summer. In winter, due to low temperatures, extra energy is required.

0643 This 20-foot gallery that follows the principles of the Trombe wall joins the main volume of the home with the guest wing. According to this principle, solar radiation penetrates the home, has an impact on the wall that, due to its thermal properties, heats up and later releases the energy in the form of heat.

0644 The pond on this property acts as a cooling element in summer, thanks to the convection of air generated from water evaporation. The cantilevers over the sliding doors provide protection from the summer sun, while in the winter, the sunlight falls on the concrete flooring with a high thermal mass.

0645 The architect of this building wanted to adapt the construction to the climate and topology of Reunion Island, where it is located. For this reason, he opted for a light structure and a covering made from PE mesh that creates a microclimate in the interior of the home and facilitates cross ventilation.

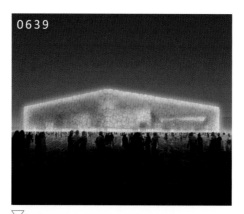
0639

0640

0641

0642

0543

0544

0645

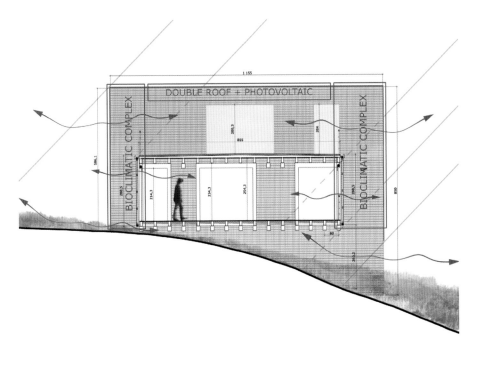

DOUBLE ROOF + PHOTOVOLTAIC

BIOCLIMATIC COMPLEX

BIOCLIMATIC COMPLEX

Bioclimatic diagram

0646 In order to guarantee a peaceful and quiet environment for the reception area of this building, an open vaulted space was created to absorb the sound, then the gap between the false ceiling and the structure was filled with soundproof material.

0647 The ceiling and 9.8-foot-high walls of this recording studio are entirely covered with units of acoustic insulation material. Each of these units treats the sound in different ways: some absorb high frequencies and some low, and the façade has been covered with a discreet blue cotton fabric.

0648 As well as containing sources of indirect lighting, the rectangular units fitted along the length of the wall, have sheets of insulating material incorporated to absorb excess high and low frequency sound, to ensure the correct recording of sound in the studio.

0649 In this recording studio the loudspeakers are completely built in to the wall. As the walls had to be totally covered, panels had to be installed to channel light indirectly from a skylight.

0650 The Spigo Group company sells construction system models made from decorative wood panels. These are easily installed in auditoriums, conference rooms, theaters, etc., and they come in a wide variety of finishes such as melamine, wood-veneers, lacquers and natural wood.

0651 A range of acoustic insulation measures are used to soundproof office spaces. When combined, these measures provide a high noise absorption capacity as required by new technical building regulations.

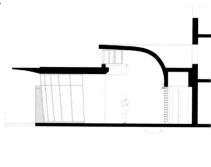

Section

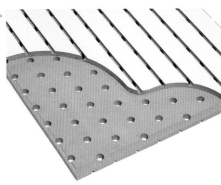

550

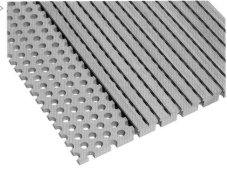

Sections

551

0652 This type of material, used in carpets and rugs, perfectly absorbs sound. It has been manufactured through a process that combines industrial and handcrafted techniques. It consists of unique wool fibers that are used for aesthetic, architectural and functional purposes.

0653 In the reception at the Wisby convention center in Sweden, a sound-absorbing panel was installed, manufactured of grey wool felt with tassels. The proportions of the panel are 27.5 × 35.4 × 385.8 inches. This model is distributed by the company Lomakka.

0654 The product Voices has been launched as independent, hanging pieces of fabric. In addition to its decorative function, it is used to absorb all the noise created in a meeting room. It is made from silk, wool and linen thread in blue and grey.

0655 Sediphone is a blown acoustic absorbent made from a base of pigmented plaster without asbestos, mineral fibers or abrasive elements. This material can be used on any type of surface area and it can replace traditional false or reinforced roofs as acoustic insulation.

0656 In this restaurant, the product Antifon is used together with flat fabric panels as acoustic insulation. The company Lomakka created different models of the same product. They can be differentiated from each other thanks to smaller or thicker loops and vice versa.

0657 These panels are made from a base of low density glass fiber sheets. They are framed in a galvanized pane, made by the company Notson. The front is finished with strips of aluminum. These Isomalla panels are highly efficient acoustic insulation for noisy machinery.

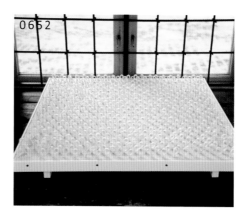

558

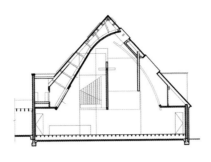

0658 Acoustic cement blocks have been used to remodel the interior of this Presbyterian church. The blocks offer the same constructive characteristics as a traditional cement block but they have surprising acoustic qualities, an unbeatable absorption coefficient and a high insulation index.

0659 In this office, the walls and the furniture are covered with a high technology fabric, and the surfaces of the walls are smooth. This combination creates a level of acoustic comfort and generates new optical and tactile stimuli. Because it absorbs sound, the room tolerates a louder concentration of noise.

0660 In this restaurant, the architects wanted to create zones with varying degrees of intimacy. In this Moroccan-style private room, red foam panels have been installed that sound-proof the room and create a relaxed atmosphere.

0661 In the private areas of this restaurant, bamboo panel walls have been installed. This acoustic insulation system enables guests to be shielded from the noise in the other restaurant spaces, and they can enjoy their privacy.

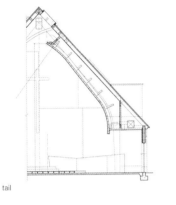

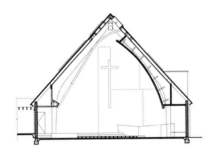

tail

Sections

659

0660

0661

0662

Side elevation

0664

0663

0665

0662 The Kiel Triangle Plaza is a small passageway that leads to an office area and an events arena. It features lit panels that continuously change color and emit water mist to create special effects.

0663 These street lights designed by the Andorran studio Arteks have an amazingly organic, almost tree-like shape and enable both sides of the piece to be illuminated. The artificially-rusted iron finish reduces the potential for weather or vandalism-related damage.

0664 The faceted glass balustrade of this bridge lights up by night. The lighting creates a kaleidoscopic effect of colors on the river down below. The bridge is a symbol that alludes to a Portuguese legend in which a crown prince and his beloved were tragically separated.

0665 These elegant metal luminaries protect the light source from potential acts of vandalism by means of a mesh.

0666 In this square, the landscape architects wanted to give back the to the space its qualities as a place of meeting and communication. To achieve this, more than 1,800 illuminated glass blocks have been inserted in the pavement. They are inset with words that have been translated into all six official languages of the European Union.

0667 The lighting along the entranceway of this Norwegian building consists of a string of beacon-shaped lights that project two spotlights for each cylindrical structure. This light is filtered and goes perfectly with the illumination on the building's façade, which emphasizes its scale.

0667

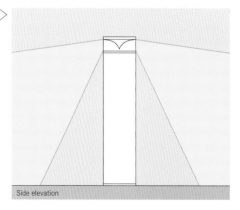

Side elevation

0668

0669

0671

0670

0672

0673

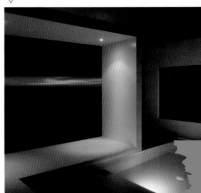

0668 The installation of small transparent illuminated cubes on an outdoor patio, or in a passageway or park, is a good atmospheric and focal solution. This type of lighting allows certain areas to stand out without projecting intense light.

0669 The Ricardo Bofill Taller de Arquitectura project, carried out in the tourist port of Savona, Italy, required studied exterior lighting. The chosen streetlamps were the Lamparaalta, which light up the seafront of this tourist city.

0670 The Latina streetlamp has become a feature of the Rotterdam seafront. For the design, the distinctive character of one of the cities most important districts was taken into account. This lighting gives the city a recognizable individual identity.

0671 For the indoor patios in the tourist port of Savona, streetlamps with a focal light were chosen. The lights are strategically positioned: they light up the benches and green areas.

0672 Spotlights have been strategically positioned on the exterior of this riverside home to provide a sense of drama. The lighting has been located in an ad hoc manner and it outlines a continuous path that it follows the semi circumference of the floor.

0673 On the exterior of this home a series of points of lights have been used. Small spotlights have been installed in a line, on the structure of the entrance, which doubles as a porch. In addition, lights have also been placed on the base that elevates the home that focally illuminate the surrounding lawn.

0674 In this Australian shopping district, a series of original backless benches has been created. As the benches do not directly sit on the ground, lighting has been placed in the space between to light the pavement at night.

0675 This walkway on the River Hai has a controlled lighting system that changes depending on the time of day and therefore saves energy. With regards to its decorative aspect, different atmospheres can be created by varying the lighting on the different stretches of the walkway.

0676 Five large structures that act as light sources provide light to this plaza. These are designed to reduce energy use and to reach a lighting capacity similar to that of large stadiums during public events.

0677 Three 52.4-foot-high poles support a set of lighting devices of different colors. A stainless steel mesh on each of the towers serves to diffuse the strength of the light.

0678 Sheets of frosted glass running horizontally along the length of this entrance lobby hide a series of flourescent tubes, which provide dim indirect lighting, which is nice in contrast with the dark granite finish.

0679 Designed by the Agence Jouin Manku studio, the purpose of these lamps was to bring intensity to the spaces they occupy. Suspended 9.8 feet in the air, they were made using thin teak strips – to match the wood paneling or the walls – that allow light to filter through their "veins".

0680 Made with a frame of stiffened wire and covered with a white, translucent textured acrylic, these lamps are not the main lighting source, but they do help to create a warm and bright atmosphere.

0681 The neon light fixtures in the common areas of this health club are elegantly inset into the suspended ceiling, without visible studs or fasteners. This solution perfectly matches the futuristic design of the interior spaces, with their abundance of straight lines and sharp angles.

0682 The interiors of this house designed by Axel Nieberg are enhanced by the warmth provided by the many sources of indirect lighting. Many of the points where the walls and furniture meet hide niches where long flourescent tubes have been inserted, with spectacular results.

0683 The rectangular columns breaking the expanse of this island bar feature are faced with sheets of matt laminated glass. The columns contain powerful halogen spotlights which turn them into striking light sources, like magic lanterns.

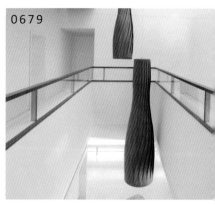

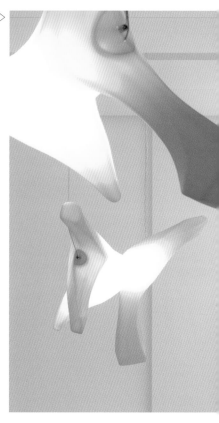

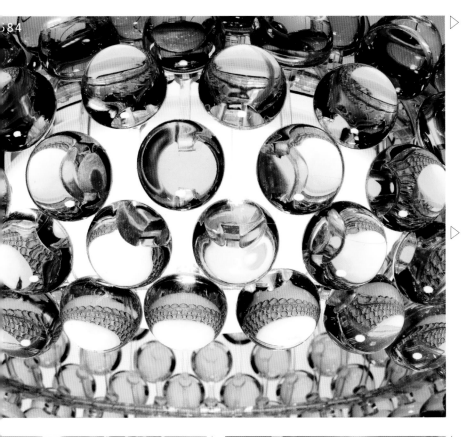

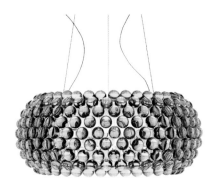

0684 The Caboche Parete wall sconce by Foscarini is made up of clear polymethacrylate balls. Matt glass panels focus the light upward and downward and filter its 230 W of halogen light throughout the room.

0685 Bamboo was the inspiration behind the creation of the lighting design in the lobby of this block of apartments. The glass structures containing halogen lights create a large labyrinth-like sculpture.

0686 The Tropico pendant lamp, an original design by Giulio Iacchetti, features a modular system that offers the possibility of creating lamps in different shapes and sizes. Repetition of the same module produces a light with a wealth of mood effects and shadows.

0687 The unsettling interior of this performance space by Daniel Libeskind is forcefully replicated in its lighting design. A number of wider than usual flourescent tube housings runs over the surface of the suspended ceiling in a somewhat uncontrolled manner, creating sharp angles and breaking off violently.

0688 The light fixtures in this stairwell, designed by Andreas Hild and Dionys Ottl, are variations on a very simple theme: the rectangular glass shade hides a halogen spotlight inside, doing away with the need for complex installations.

0689 Use has been made of the niches created along the length of the walls and on the sides of the lowest part of the ceiling in this kitchen to install continuous sources of indirect lighting, with truly incredible results.

0690 The spectacular effects of the indirect flourescent lights installed in this hotel create the feeling that the walls are painted in phosphorescent colors, when in reality they are just lit up that way.

0691 The use of low-energy light bulbs in Terminal 4 of the Madrid-Barajas airport was part of the strategy for bioclimatic design and the measures, both active and passive, adopted by the architects. In particular, mirrors were used to optimize illumination.

0692 The Gucchi lamp is a modular unit expressly designed by the architects Schwarz Design for the communal areas of this house. The same design has been installed in various sizes, by adding a larger number of acrylic panels.

0693 The tempered steel structure supporting the votive candles has a lower platform with an area to catch the dripping wax, and an upper platform where the candles are kept. It was first designed for a renovated church, but it can also be used for large residences with their own small chapels.

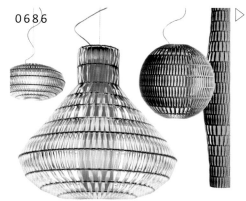

0686

0687

0688

Suspension system drawings

0689

0590

0691

0692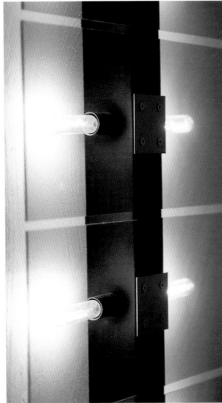

0693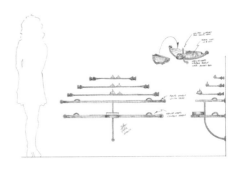

Drawing of the votive candle support frame

0694

0695

Assembled dwelling diagram

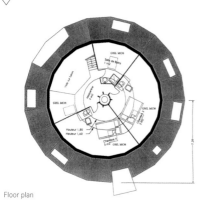

0696

Floor plan

0697

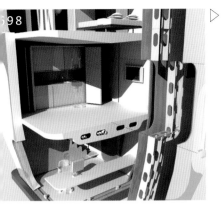

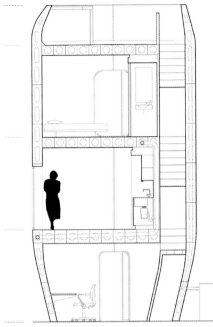

Section

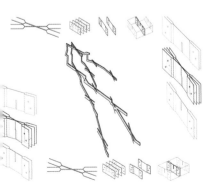

ribs axonometric

0694 This project was created for the launch of the PlayStation 3 in the UK. The designers created an interactive installation using 46 columns with LED lights, a speaker and a sound channel for each terminal. The movement of visitors caused a crossfire of light and sound.

0695 Due to the use of photovoltaic solar panels, an Icinene foam insulation system and air conditioning from a heat pump, the energy consumption of this prefabricated house is 30% less than in traditionally-built homes.

0696 This wooden home, located in Brittany, France, boasts the unusual feature that it rotates 320° both in the same direction as the sun and in the opposite direction. The system, either manual or remote control, is precursor to what we know today as automated. The angle of the turn and the speed can be adjusted automatically using software.

0697 The use of new technologies also boils down to small details. The architect Luis de Garrido chose to equip the R4 House, on display in Construmat 2007, with the latest Miele electrical appliances: low water and energy consumption washing machine and energy-efficient kitchen.

0698 The exterior and the interior finishes of this home are inspired by the technology used for the wings of an airplane; the skin is rigid, compact but at the same time light. The assembly of eight aluminum panels (7.9 × 30 feet) enables the creation a smaller module of a home. Each module occupies 258 square feet.

0699 The temperature of the interior of this home is managed by hot/cold radiant flooring, which is considered to be one of the best systems that exists today for energy efficiency. An automatic wireless thermostat system regulates the temperature of each room individually.

0700 The basis for the construction of this residence consisted of a series of 1-inch-wide plywood ribs cut by laser. Each rib was numbered and cut according to its position. The Burst* designs offer different solutions and are an alternative to mass production models.

0701 This project in Zushi, Japan, involved exploring the constructive and formal possibilities of wood panels developed by Yasuhiro Yamashita in collaboration with Jyo-Ko the structural engineer. These panels act as structure, thermal insulator and damp-proof material, and also function as finishing.

0702 This home in Barcelona has a glass façade with a metallic outer skin of four modules in a block facing each other. They serve as protection from the sun and possible inclemencies of weather. The block is opened automatically by a hydraulic engine supported by rubber belts.

0703 Chris Bosse specializes in projects that connect architecture to the virtual world. The Paradise Pavilion, designed for the Entry 06 exposition in Germany, presents biomorphic forms designed using different software systems. Their inspiration is taken from natural forms to create architectural structures.

0704 This residence in Tasmania has a rainwater collection system for domestic use and a system to treat greywater through a process of septic tanks and filtering. Due to the remote location of the home it is not connected to the supply and sewer network.

0705 This commercial building of three floors plus the hall sustained by V-shaped pillar foundations, presents a façade formed by a series of transparent pneumatic panels, with membranes that stretch owing to the tension exerted by the diagonal beams. The general look of the façade is "padded".

0706 Through the use of a screen of acrylic panels, this 5,380-square-foot installation, which was commissioned by the magazine *Interior Design* and the NeoCon West fair, served as an aesthetic and technological counterpoint so that exhibition attendees could consult their email while they took a break or a coffee.

0707 The rooms in this hotel have LCD screens behind the glass sliding doors of the closets, and are equipped with a webcam system. According to the designers, this service was added to combat the feeling of loneliness that some guests suffer when they are in hotels.

0708 The façade of the swimming competition pavilion for the Beijing 2008 Olympics Games reminds us of the natural composition of organic cells. The outer skin is made up of EFTE (ethylene tetrafluroetylene), a transparent plastic polymer that adapts to adverse climate conditions.

0709 The winding corridors of this hotel are lit up with an LED RGB system pre-programmed to synchronize with the different times of the day: dim lights at night and bright colors during the day. Each floor of the hotel has a predetermined color: yellow, green, orange or black. The general design combines art, technology and modernity.

0710 This installation was displayed in the windows of the Wellcome Trust foundation in London, an association for the improvement of the quality of human life. The arms are a symbol of medical research. The skin "disappears" as if it were subject to X-rays, so that you can see the veins and arteries lit up electronically.

0711 TheANEMIX is a new lighting system based on the three-dimensional effect and inspired by bioluminescence. Comprised of a luminous panel with an aluminum frame, it is made up of a luminous layer and then a reflective layer that can be modified to create different effects.

0703

Rendering

0704

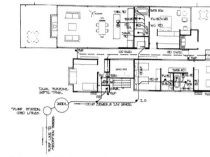

Rainwater and black water drainage scheme

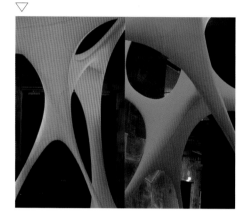

0705

0706

0707

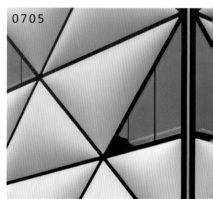

0708

0709

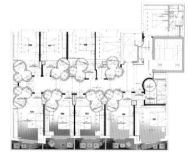

General ground floor plan

0712

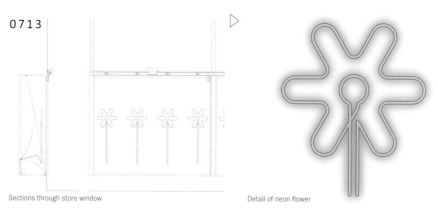

0713

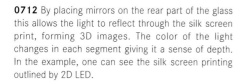

Sections through store window

Detail of neon flower

0714

0712 By placing mirrors on the rear part of the glass this allows the light to reflect through the silk screen print, forming 3D images. The color of the light changes in each segment giving it a sense of depth. In the example, one can see the silk screen printing outlined by 2D LED.

0713 These technical plans correspond to the installation carried out for the Häagen-Dazs window display in the New York stores. It was made of 21 neon flowers, fitted with movement sensors. When a passer-by walked by, the corresponding flower lit up and the sound of a carillon was heard.

0714 This interactive wall tries to be, according to the designers of the Delft Architecture Faculty, a prototype emotional architectural element. The project was funded by Festo — a leading company in technology for pneumatics and electrical automation — for its Festo Bionic knowledge network.

0715 For this Chanel store in the Ginza in Tokyo, Peter Marino designed a façade made from multiple layers of liquid crystal. Through a 6,000 pixel system lit up by programmable LED, images of the brand are projected during the night as well as abstract urban forms. During the day transparency reigns.

0716 This wall responds to the movement of people. It is made of seven panels that independently curve forward or backward and has LED lights that illuminate more or less depending on the proximity of passers-by. The wall also emits sound: the more synchronised the movements the slower the sounds.

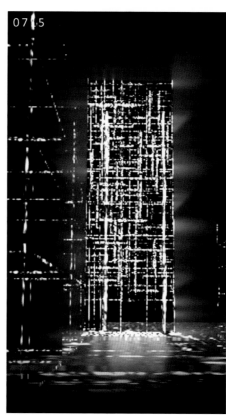

0715

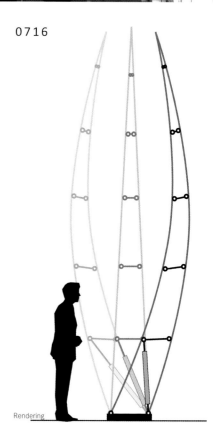

0716

Rendering

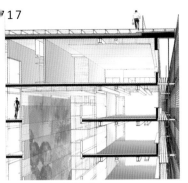

...tion through cube with light displays

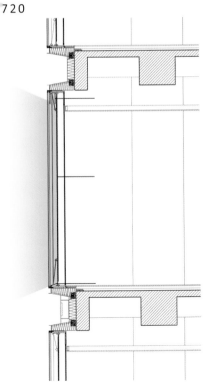

...ction through wall with reflector system

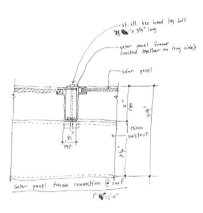

Construction detail of the panel and Unistrut metal framing

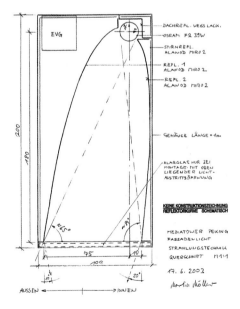

Curve diagram of light reflection

0717 This lighting system is based on glass tubes that contain LED, which give off light flows from the red, green, blue color spectrum according to an Euclidian geometry order. The plasma fractals are created through flows of algorithms that emerge from the four ends of the sides of the cube.

0718 The Solar Umbrella House in Venice, California, drew inspiration from the Umbrella House (1953) by Paul Rudolph and involves the extension of the existing residence. The roof of this extension is covered with solar panels that provide 100% of energetic consumption. The detail shows the layout of the panel with its Unistrut anchorage system.

0719 The structure of the house is formed by prefabricated panels framed by the prestressed steel profiles; the laminated wooden panels measure 4.7 × 28.3 × 118.1 to 196.8 inches and are assembled onsite. The clients, a young couple, wanted a formal, unusual design for their home.

0720 The lighting for this large book and multimedia store in northeast Beijing is made up of a LED display that surrounds the building and allows moving text messages to be sent out. The layout of large, transparent glass panels that can be darkened allows for images to be sent out by retroprojection.

0721 The façade, in addition to the skin of the wall, has a giant screen. It is made up of more than 16,000 windows created as a pixel monitor, capable of representing 256 shades of grey that can change their level of brightness up to 24 times per second. The diagram shows the reflection of the light on the camera created between the two panes of glass that make up the transparent panel of the windows.

0722

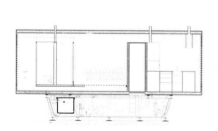

Longitudinal section

0724

0723

727

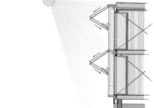

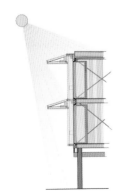

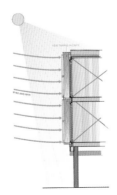

Sun exposure diagrams

0722 This prefabricated module was built in a factory by the firm Capa for presentation at the construction industry fair Concreta 2003. It is designed as a residential unit, commercial space or exhibition use. The photovoltaic panels, which can be positioned automatically, occupy an area of 194 square feet and store enough energy to last for three days.

0723 Fixed to a system of rails, the folding slatted panel is lowered to protect this restaurant from the sun, or is raised to function as a canopy for the terrace by means of a mechanical operation.

0724 Taking into account the intense sun and heat of this part of Malaysia, the architects of this residence though it appropriate to install a system where a part of the sunshades act as brise-soleil to cover the façade that could be raised and lowered automatically.

0725 The peculiarity of this house is its ability to rotate towards the sun. This operation is considered to be the precursor of current domotic systems. Rotation can be manual or automated, enabling the speed of rotation to be adjusted, and an angle of up to 320°.

0726 Biceberg is an automatic, intelligent underground parking system that receives and returns bicycles to the street in under 30 seconds and that allows you to store other equipment such as your backpack and helmet. To use it you must have a Biceberg membership.

0727 The folding louvers on the main façade protect against wind and rain, and mean that the solar heat accumulates in the space between the folding louvers and doors inside during the winter days. Raised in summer, they allow cross-ventilation.

0728 The old headquarters of the Brussels water company was transformed into a complex of offices and homes. The homes are located in the highest part of the tower where the old concrete skin was substituted for steel and glass. They can be accessed by an elevator.

0729 Approximately 50% of the perimeter of this house is covered with adjustable slats of wood that provide sun protection and control the amount of daylighting entering the house. On warmer days, the slats are controlled by a computer system that rotates them automatically according to the angle of solar incidence.

0730 This project was displayed at the Objet Public exhibition in the Pavillon de l'Arsenal in Paris. Two students from the Malaquais School designed an elevator system for bicycle parking. The metal structure can be adapted to most walls.

0731 This new auditorium in Breda has a total area of 7,750 square feet and is an extension of the adjacent building of 9,470 square feet, which was also renovated. The main entrance has a dual pivoting door, while the service entrance is to one side to provide access for cargo and construction trucks.

0732 Energy criteria were important in the renovation of this 1960s building in Salzburg. The façade therefore contains fiberglass insulation in the walls, double glazing and pivoting, and motorized shutters.

0733 This small wedding chapel in Kobuchizawa, Japan, is made from two large leaves: one of steel and the other of glass. When the groom sees the face of his bride, the steel structure mechanically rises up, revealing the pond. The leaf weighs 11 tons and takes 38 seconds to open.

0734 The 1,053-foot glass roof of the Central Station of Berlin is formed by a glazed grid roof that runs east-west over a steel structure. This length was shortened to 361 feet because of time constraints. The central grids can be opened mechanically.

0735 The red lines in the diagram indicate the vertical movement of the mobile window in the entrance area of the house in Venice Beach. The space created between these walls was used to place pivoting windows that allow the Pacific Ocean breezes to be regulated throughout the house.

0728

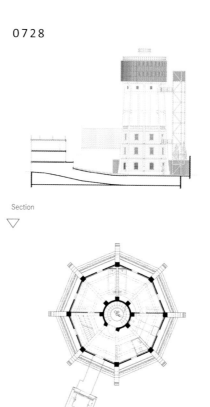

Section

Floor plan

0729

0730

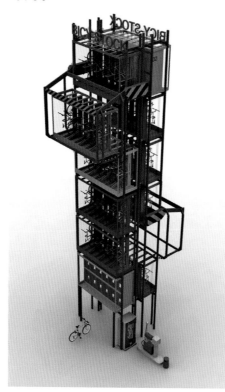

0731

32

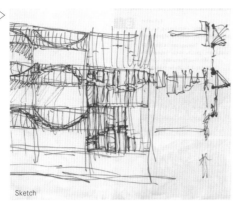

Sketch

0733

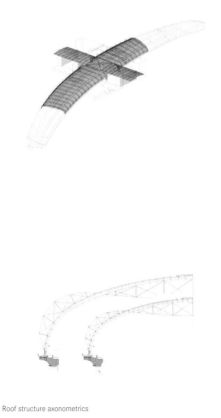

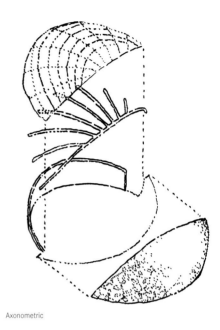

Axonometric

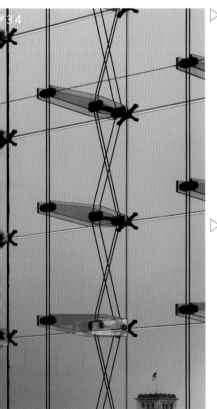

34

0735

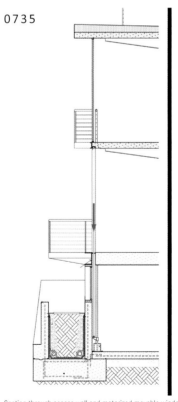

Roof structure axonometrics

Section through access wall and motorized movable window system

0736

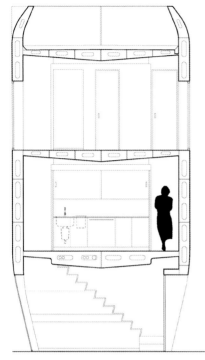

Section

0737

0738

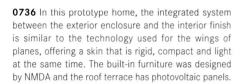

Sketches

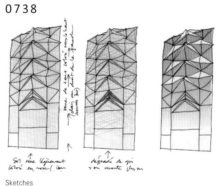

0739

0736 In this prototype home, the integrated system between the exterior enclosure and the interior finish is similar to the technology used for the wings of planes, offering a skin that is rigid, compact and light at the same time. The built-in furniture was designed by NMDA and the roof terrace has photovoltaic panels.

0737 The Photonics center is laid out in modules, which contain the different laboratories, production areas and offices. The interiors have been designed to meet the building's functional needs. For example, the area containing the optical laboratories requires a permanent state of shade.

0738 For this Citroën showroom, red, as a perfect symbol of the brand, is an essential part of the design in both the central rotating platform and the glazed façade which contains red-stained sections that filter the sunlight.

0739 The self-sustaining glass roof of this greenhouse is fixed by nodes (200 in total) braced on four points. Each node is attached to the structure. To achieve the vaulted or double-curved geometry, the structure has been laser cut and folded according to a curve radius in three dimensions.

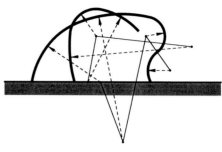

Preliminary study

0741

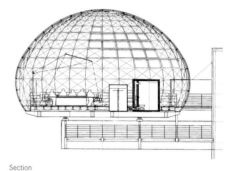

Section

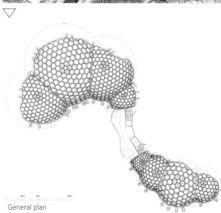

General plan

0740 Shuhei Endo designed this railway station using an industrial material, galvanized steel, and challenging non-Euclidean geometry through three-dimensional processes. Benches, chairs and bicycle parking have been provided for users among the modules.

0741 This ball is located at the top of the Lingotto multi-function center, a mixed-use space created after a renovation of a former Fiat car plant. The completely transparent ball affords views over the Alps and the hills surrounding Torino.

0742 Advanced glass construction techniques were used to construct this shell greenhouse in Malmö. The glass skin, suspended by steel arches, is completely untreated, and has a surface area of 1,290 square feet, a volume of 31,430 cubic feet, a length of 72 feet, and a height of 34.5 feet.

0743 The structure of the Project Eden sphere, a botanical center that exhibits the Earth's biological diversity, was designed to capture the maximum amount of solar radiation. At night, the back walls of the ETFE (ethylene tetrafluoroethylene) hexagons dissipate the heat accumulated during the day.

0744

0745

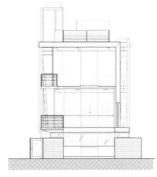

West elevation

0746

Renderings of the building skin

0747

0748

0749

0744 The main objective in the design of this culteral center was to evoke telecommunications, as that is the purpose of the structure. The glass panels are framed in cornices that cover the entire perimeter of the building. A system of mirrors placed inside allows the façade to act as a screen onto which images are projected.

0745 The shell of this building is made of aluminum panels that have a thermal insulation core made from thick synthetic foam. These panels are the type normally used in refrigeration chambers, and are secured with screws on the reinforced floors of each level.

0746 The Galleria Hall West in Seoul is an exclusive shopping mall. The shell is lined with glass discs treated with an iridescent coating that creates a façade with a constantly changing appearance. At night, the discs are illuminated by a lighting system designed by UNStudio and ArupLighting.

0747 The inspiration for the elliptical shape of the two bubbles that make up this building, suspended on stainless steel legs over a lake, was taken from distillery tanks. Inside, there are laboratories for the new research center for a brand of grappa. The steps have fluorescent lights.

0748 The Randstadrail viaduct project consists of a tubular construction of 1,312 feet formed by a ring of steel with a diameter of around 33 feet. V-shaped columns support the structure, which has space inside for two lines and the trains that pass through it.

0749 This 460-foot pedestrian tunnel, which connects the Wilhelminaplein railway station and the Luxor Theater, has great interior visibility. The computer-monitored tunnel lighting gradually changes color.

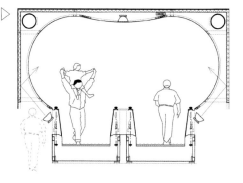

Section

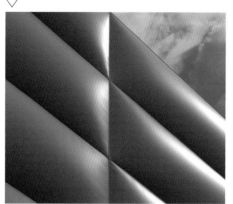

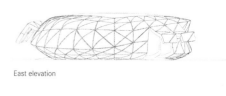

East elevation

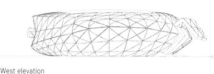

West elevation

0750 This 36,274 square foot temporary building for BMW at the IAA fair of Frankfurt consists of 166 air-filled membranes, measuring 6.5 × 49 feet that are kept at a certain pressure with the use of a compressor. The building can be dismantled in seven days.

0751 ONL, with a definite tendency towards 3D designs, reformulated the WEB pavilion used during the Floriade international exhibition. This space was dismantled, renamed iWEB, and assembled in front of the Delft Faculty of Architecture. It is now a space for meetings and a workshop for Protospace researchers.

0752 For this luxury hotel in Rioja Alavesa, Frank O. Gehry designed a building of undulating forms, made possible thanks to the titanium plates that form part of the cantilevers. Some of the walkways are surrounded by the steel structure and glass divider walls.

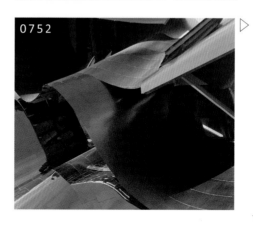

0753 For this 12,915-square-foot Citroën showroom, located on the Champs-Elysées, Gautrand created a design inspired by a transmission belt. The building is arranged on seven floors plus a basement that has a rotating platform in the center, where the cars are exhibited.

0754 The façade of this luxury car dealership consists of 300 glass panels set within a steel structure. Internally, the four floors form a closed loop following the curves of the front façade. The design is a response to three-dimensional models.

0755 The renovation of the façade and interior of the Galleria Hall West was completed in 2004. For the new façade, 4,330 glass discs were laid over metal cladding that was placed over the building's former skin. The client wanted the new skin to have a modern and unique character.

0756 This glass cube is made of glass, aluminum, acrylic and polyurethane panels. These are all technical materials that are considered hi-tech materials from the 21st century. In a formal comparison, the striations on the exterior façade and interior panels have an extremely organic aspect.

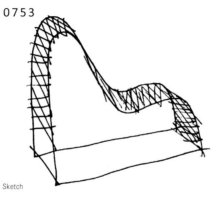

Sketch

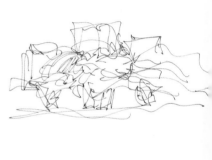

Sketches

0754

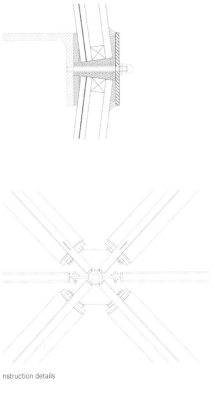

0755

0756

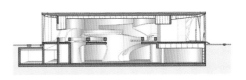

nstruction details

Cross section

0757 The Urbia furniture expansion system for small residential spaces was designed with two aims: to provide storage space and offer clients pieces that could be dismantled and taken to new homes. The unit is designed using hollow wood panels and independent modules to offer maximum structural performance.

0758 The spectacular fireplace in this residence designed by Emil Urbel features an amazingly original accessory: the space for storing firewood is no more than an elegant rectangle dug into the living room floor.

0759 These blackbox modular shelving units have a striking exterior finish in padded leather. This becomes a decorative feature when the unit is closed. The books hidden inside come into view when the structure is opened out.

0760 The design of this residence, the work of 123DV, features the intention of turning the walls into a fundamental part of the furniture. By bringing them forward to give them more depth, a series of niches offer elegant storage spaces.

Section

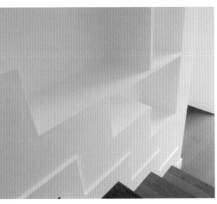

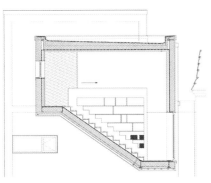

staircase section

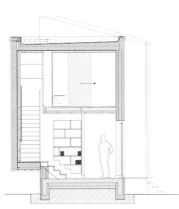

0761 To make more efficient use of the space in a loft apartment of under 538 square feet, Behles & Jochimsen designed an amusing bright pink central island, providing ample storage space. It contains the sink and range, and fold-out drawers. The sliding doors to the passageway are also hidden away inside its structure.

0762 This residence designed by Petra Petersson surprises with the good use it makes of space. An example of this is the intelligent use of space on the internal staircase wall, which becomes a large storage area for books and objects.

0763 Occupying a small room in this recently remodeled residence, the closet stands out in the intelligent use it makes of space and for the elegance with which the drawers are arranged, enabling the drawer pulls to become a decorative feature.

0764 The slender design of these lockers features a close-to-metallic color that fits perfectly into their surroundings. The shape of the handles and the simplicity of the plinth-like bench are outstanding features.

0765 Made-to-measure bookshelves make the best use of the available space and the height of the walls, and adapt to the eaves and projections of the walls. It is essential to adapt the dimensions of the bookshelves to the available space and its intended use, in order to be able to work comfortably.

0766 This architectural structure with sloping ceilings and columns has made best use of the space left at the lowest end of the sloped ceiling, by fitting cupboards into the area, and using the columns to frame a storage cupboard, which separates the two areas of the dining room.

0767 Closing off bookshelves with sliding doors means that the contents can be hidden from prying eyes, or objects can simply be stored when not in use. If you are storing collections or ornaments, completely or partially enclosing them with glass doors that act as windows, allows the contents to be lit up.

0768 The most visually weightless storage system is one that attaches to the wall, particularly if it is in the form of metal or glass shelves. This also allows for uninhibited and original designs like these studio bookshelves designed by Desalto.

0763

0764

0765

0766

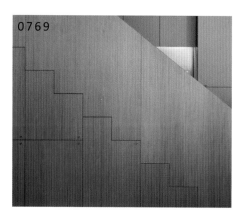

0769

0770

0771

0772

0769 Stairwells offer many storage possibilities: fitting anything from a coat stand to a chest of drawers, a sofa-bed or even a system of built-in cupboards, as shown in this example.

0770 Inside houses, there are occasionally different levels between spaces that are connected using units or structures. These areas can be converted into the perfect support for drawers, boxes, books, cleaning products or any kind of small container.

0771 In a corridor that is not wide enough to fit a wall-to-floor cupboard, fitting a brightly colored, well-organized open closet is a good storage solution.

0772 When it is not possible to have a fitted closet near the entrance, small cupboards in structures connecting different spaces in a hallway or at the end of a corridor are perfect for storing coats, hats and bags.

0773 The portable office is a modern concept, made possible only thanks to advances in new technologies, and complemented by the widespread lack of space in modern homes. This original mobile study aesthetically reflects the concept of the home-office.

0774 A complete and understated work station, with everything you need on hand: drawers, CD racks, printer and photocopier under the desk, and an extendable shelf for the keyboard which frees up space on the desktop.

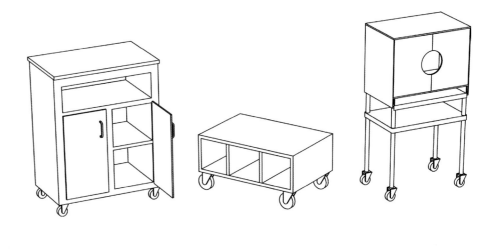

Axonometric projections

0775 The interior layout of a closet should be decided with regard to the dressing room and the needs of each user. In this way, the design offered by MOVE/ DARAQ Import offers optimal organization and systematization of the closet.

0776 The dressing room, once all of the closets are fitted, should be wide enough to be used comfortably. Normally, a space of around 3 feet wide is sufficient. Having a chair at the back of a corridor-shaped dressing room, as in this case, makes it easier to get dressed and undressed.

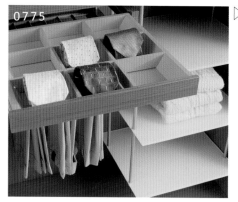

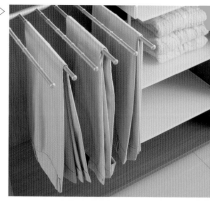

0777

0778

▷

0779

0780

▽

0777 Made-to-measure furniture can adapt to the most irregular of structures, and makes it possible to gain valuable storage space, such as drawers under a couch or cupboards made to adapt to variations in the walls, such as columns or inclines.

0778 In this narrow house, all of the partitions have been removed to create a single integrated environment, with a large closet along the entire length of the floor, providing much-needed storage space.

0779 Sometimes, the structure of a staircase can be used to fit shelves at various heights, made from the same material as the wall they are attached to.

0780 Portable desks that are compact and sometimes even foldable, can also provide a solution to the need for small, mobile and discreet working areas. In this case, Kabalab has created a foldable wooden desk.

0781 For DecorGem wall coverings, Omnidecor developed an exclusive process technology for high-temperature fusion of glass or tile to a color print, resulting in cheerful floral motifs.

0782 This bathroom is a separate environment from the bedroom, but is visually connected. This is thanks to a large glazed screen that by night has a sparkling amber frame. The same effect is repeated on the ceiling of the bedroom and around the bathtub.

0781

0782

0784

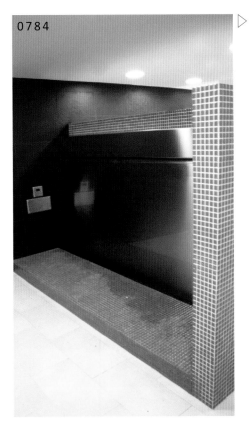

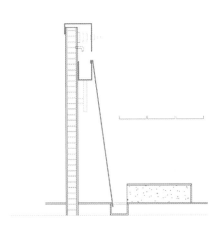

Section

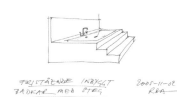

85

FRISTÅENDE INBYGGT
BADKAR MED STEG

2005-11-02
RBA

0783 This shower cubicle allows the door to operate like the door to the room, adding a striking, stylized look and a shiny steel finish to the design.

0784 This design by Elisabet Faura, Gerard Veciana, and Esther Pascual applies an increasingly fashionable decorative solution for public rest rooms. A 0.2-inch-thick stainless steel sheet is positioned with the right slope to fit over a channel in the plinth, covered with the same tiles as the frame of the structure.

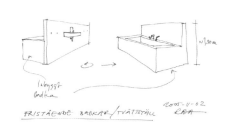

86

Inbyggt
Badkar

FRISTÅENDE BADKAR / TVÄTTSTALL

2005-11-02
RBA

Sketches

0785 The solid block of black granite in the center of the 538-square-foot bathroom contains the bath and in the area behind, a wooden wash basin. In order to create a sense of space, both the shower and the sauna are marked by a screen and glass walls.

0786 Small square mosaic tiles are an increasingly popular material for lining bathroom walls. If the same color is also chosen for the floor, the result can be even more striking.

0787 A system of cupboards and shelves serves as decoration at the entrance to this bathroom and provides storage for small objects, since the two stone bases used to construct the hand basin do not provide sufficient space.

0788 The master bathroom has views that give those living there the sensation of being in the middle of the woods. The onyx colored surfaces and the ergonomic lounge located inside the glass-paneled shower are the most remarkable features of this bathroom.

0789 The main features of this en suite bathroom are a mixture of finishes, an absence of ornamentation and a highly functional layout. The space, which can be seen from the stairs, forms part of the sleeping area and consists of a closet, a large shower with a deck, sanitary fixtures and a small bath with an adjoining hand basin.

0790 In this bathroom, the pure and elemental lines of architecture are complemented by the minimalist aesthetics such as the expanse of gray stone and pink glass that invite one to relax. The pool/bath has a tray to collect any overflow water.

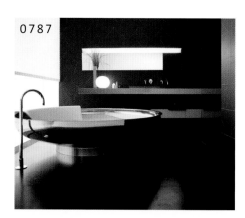

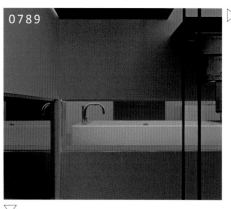

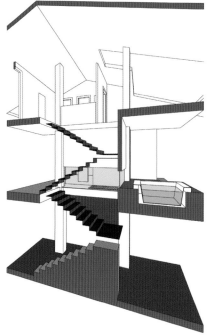

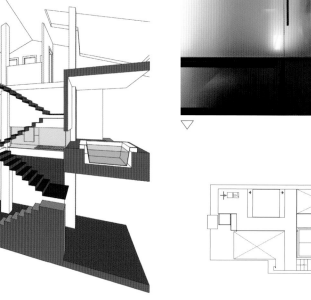

Suite plan

Section

General layout

0791 This luxury hotel suite is decorated with marble and stone on the lower half of the walls and the floor, and the rest with mosaics in grey and brown tones, by the company Bisazza. Decorative details give it a personal touch, such as the original shape of the bathtub and the lamps over the hand-basin.

0792 The many mirrored surfaces infuse these marble-covered spaces with light. The gold and neutral tones create a deliberate contrast with the blue color in the rest of the spaces and prevent it from becoming monotonous.

0793 The placement of differently colored mosaic tiles arranged in stripes personalizes this bathroom. The tub has been inset into the floor to visually free up space.

0794 The design of the Opera model by Toscoquattro is based on ebony wood with finishes in white Corian, creating a comfortable and elegant atmosphere.

0795 Made-to-measure furniture makes it possible to use all the available space in a bathroom to the best advantage, adapting to the style of the house and the available space, without overloading it.

0796 It is the location of the toilet and sink that makes this bathroom really original: they are located in different areas of the house. This is due to the fact that the building has maintained the original architectural structure of its previous incarnation, a garage.

0797 This bathroom has various remarkable design features, but most notable is the fact that black completely dominates. The owner wanted to feel "as if she was in a Shanghai bar". The bathtub is on a black mosaic platform.

0798 This bathroom, integrated into the master bedroom, is separated by a partition that gives it an almost sculptural look. Inspired by a sheet of paper, the design uses the APRA fold as the basis for the countertop complete with a sink and mirror.

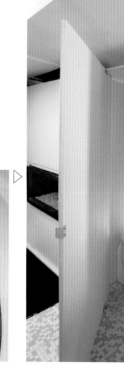

97

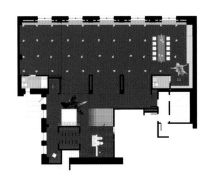

General layout

98

0799

0800

0801

0802

0799 The visual and physical separation between the sanitary fixtures and the sink is created by the construction of a low wall and by a pair of cupboards placed at right angles to the wall, as in the example of this Duravit design.

0800 A metal structure has been created to house the bathroom. It has two functions: on one side, this wall demarcates the space for the toilet, and on the other it provides the necessary privacy required by this area of the loft.

0801 There are various options for fitting a storage space underneath the sink in a bathroom with pure lines: a tailor-made surface along the entire wall; a simple shelf; a minimalist unit; or a cantilever cupboard just at the right height to hide the drain pipes, as in this case.

0802 The bathroom in this home is part of a tube-shaped wooden-veneered structure that continues into the bedroom and forms part of the bed. The rich mosaic interior is separated from the outside by the curved amber-colored glass walls.

0803 This bathroom's walls are covered with Snowflake mosaics by Bisazza, which contrast the smooth, natural tones of the surfaces of the bathtub and shower. The faucets on the sink and shower are industrial-style and have original heart-shaped openings.

0804 Without completely separating the environments in this home, the architect has chosen to hide the sanitary fixtures, and separate the shower and bathtub area. Clear or frosted glass partitions are perfect for this, as they create individual areas without decreasing the size of the space.

0803

0804

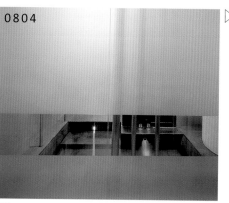

0805

0806

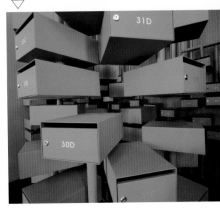

0805 The lobby of The Cove Atlantis hotel resembles a temple. Underneath high wood ceilings there is a corridor with stone pillars and cylindrical brass lamps. Each of these structures features a niche that houses aluminum sculptures.

0806 The fanned arrangement of residents' mailboxes in this apartment building is a sculptural element. The color green and bamboo-like forms inspired by nature prevail in this predominantly residential lobby.

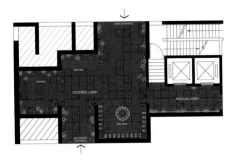

Floor plan

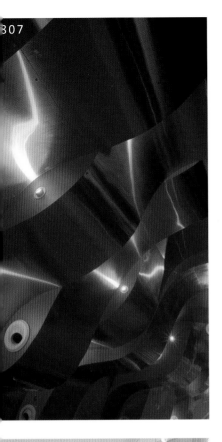

0307

0808

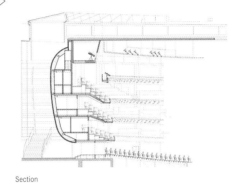

Section

809

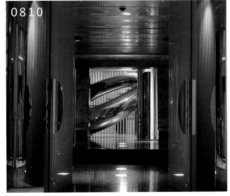

0810

Axonometric projection

0807 The Italian marble cladding that has been used to cover the walls and floor provides light and a touch of glamour to the lobby of this theater located in Mumbai. The undulating steel plates that cover part of the roof create a volume that flows and dissolves the conventional boundaries between the walls and other surfaces.

0808 This 75,350 square foot, four-story lobby features sculptural lamps designed by the artist Olafur Eliasson. These are suspended at different heights and are made up of delicate pieces of glass mounted together.

0809 The association between the old and the new is the main feature in the lobby of this hotel. This symbiosis gives rise to endless creative possibilities. The roof structure is exposed, imitating the style used in historical buildings.

0810 The lobby of this hotel is an avant-garde space with reflections, transparency and dynamism. The focal point is the reception desk, whicxh consists of a spectacular stainless steel ring that is tilted and supported on a column.

0811 A house inside a house, composed mainly of steel, glass and aluminum panels with LED lights, was installed in the lobby of the Börsenhalle, the historic seat of the Hamburg Stock Exchange. The new space houses offices, meeting rooms, and a social club.

0812 The design of this room, featuring deep red on all the surfaces, is laden with sensuality. The lobby of this Love Hotel is a far cry from the vulgar image generally associated with this type of hotel, since it has an atmosphere brimming with sensuality and minimalism.

0813 The interior design scheme of this lobby uses the company's corporate colors, white and ruby red. The reception desk and the back wall are lined with a glossy gray film. The waiting area is defined by a 4.9-foot-high curtain made from a fine fringe.

0814 The lobby of the Andorra Convention, Fair and Exhibition Center, which also houses the cafeteria, reception and cloakroom, is clearly differentiated from the other spaces with a false ceiling made from wood paneling.

0815 Stone has been used as the interior cladding on the entrance wall; this feature is echoed in other rooms in the building. Different shades of gray and orange have been used in the geometric elements featured on the walls.

0816 The lobby of the Akron Art Museum in Ohio was envisaged as a space to accommodate banquets, presentations and art festivals. Due to its volume and glazed structure, very little artificial energy is required for the climate control system.

0811

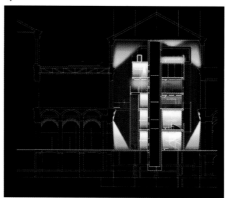

0812

0813

0814

0815

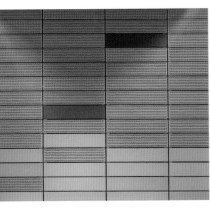

0816

0817 Traditional Roman baths were the inspiration for the structure of this spa. The rooms are sober and have a minimalist décor characterized by spaces lined in black stone. The lobby has few objects; one of its main features is a row of sand-colored benches located against one wall.

0818 The lobby of this complex of three university buildings was envisaged as an important transit area. Connections to the street have therefore been facilitated and the spaces contain benches that encourage people to meet up. Additionaly, they and are located at a height that creates a certain air of intimacy.

0819 Due to the function of this building complex – used for cultural, educational and private research purposes – the architects created meeting points to facilitate the exchange of knowledge between students and scientists.

0820 The reception area of the last edition of the Stockholm Furniture Fair was designed by Konstantin Grcic. The space consisted of a welcoming garden with plants, nets and a mixture of objects and furniture by the German designer.

0821 The space between the old building and new constructions of the Canada Ballet School was enclosed to create a lounge that forms the heart of the school. The most predominant elements used in this hall are weathered steel and a large digital screen.

0822 The lobby of this IT University was designed as a large building open to the exterior. As such the east and west façades were made up of glass screens with varying degrees of opacity. Some of the glass panels in these walls contain engravings and others can be opened as part of the lateral ventilation system.

0817

0818

0819

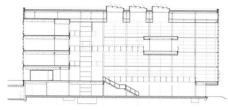

Side elevation

0820

0821

822

0823

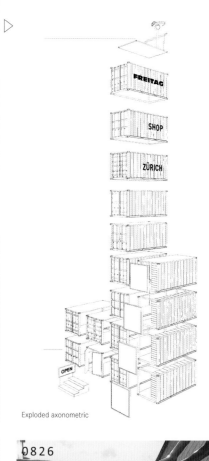

Exploded axonometric

0824

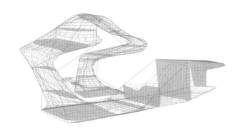

Rendering

0825

0826

0827

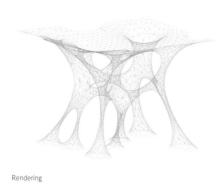

Rendering

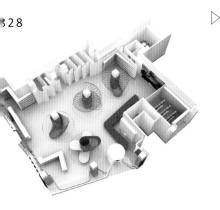

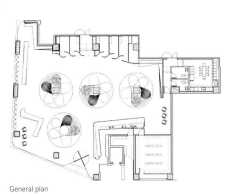

General plan

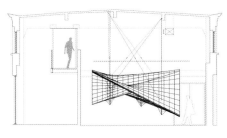

Section

0831

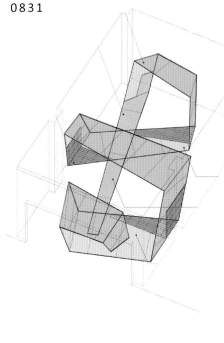

Axonometric projection

0823 This 89-foot tower located near the Freitag factory is the official sales point for this brand in Zúrich. The tower is made from 17 repurposed containers. Those responsible for the Swiss brand refer to this as a "bonsai skyscraper" and the sculptural character between the built-up areas is unquestionable.

0824 Graft designed this stand for the Sci Fi Channel at the comic and pop culture fair in San Diego, California. The structure, which evokes the shape of a giant eel, incorporates LED projection systems and three LCD screens showing the content that will be broadcast on the channel in the coming season.

0825 Chris Bosse designed this pavilion, weighing only 37.5 pounds, which was inspired by structures formed by microscopic cells. The result is irregular biomorphic shapes, similar to those in sponges and corals, which were created using different software programs.

0826 This installation is located in the inner courtyard of Nissan's design studios. The landscape architects suspended this canopy of branches, creating a shadow effect on the floor below. The branches are made of light blue fiberglass.

0827 This installation of recycled cardboard, forming a total of 3,500 molecules in two different forms, was exhibited by design students at the Sydney University of Technology. The molecules were plastered on walls, ceilings and each other, and were illuminated by fluorescent lighting.

0828 The original space on these premises, located on the ground floor of a new building of Roppongi Hills in Tokyo, included four large columns that divided the space. These are concealed by rotating bands that serve as a guide for hanging apparel and are like very light and mobile sculptures.

0829 This installation for the SCI-Arc Gallery in Los Angeles consists of a flat sculpture lined with grass; a 1,076 square foot thin and fine layer suspended by wires. This, according to the creators, expresses the dichotomy between its organic nature and highly artificial aspect.

0830 For this roof in the neighborhood of Greenwich, Graftworks used gradually sloping wooden walkways that twist to one side at the far end. These walkways combine a marked sculptural character with a comfortable appearance.

0831 This conference installation, commissioned by *Interior Design* magazine and NeoCon West, was a space where attendees could check their email, and meet to talk or relax. It consists of an orange surface which folds over itself.

0832 For the Bons Enfants ministerial building in Paris, Francis Soler committed to three measures: new lighting, a new garden and a new façade. The building, which is more than 70 years old has already undergone three interventions. The ornamental steel skin creates shadows and reflections on the façade.

0833 For the Aoyama Diesel Denim Gallery in Hiroshima, Japan, Makoto Tanijiri proposed an industrial-style installation commissioned by Masaaki Takahashi. This tube installation can be found in the interior of the gallery as if it were a tree that grows from the floor, and the latest collection of Diesel jeans hang from it.

0834 The artist Robert Owen, collaborator in the Denton Corker Marshall studio, drew inspiration from a trap for eels in the design of this bridge located in Melbourne. The base is made from concrete while the deck is made from a structure in the shape of an aboriginal fishing net suspended by oval arches.

0835 The second façade of the Light Cube in Saarbrücken consists of a system of bars distributed over two layers that form a sculptural mesh over the stainless steel skin. The bars are LED glass tubes that diffuse a large spectrum of RGB colors and medium tones.

0836 For this seasonal garden in Sydney, the architects reused previously colored used tires as planters for grass, distributed around a pedestrian area. This sculptural ensemble is an allegory aimed at encouraging the use of recycled material in urban design.

0837 The center of scenic arts in Memphis invited six architects and designers to participate in remodeling their installations. Vito Acconci, architect and sculptor opted to create shapeless structures, covered in a stainless steel skin that acts as a base, body and cover.

0838 In this seasonal installation for a cultural event in Oslo, Rintala created this design following two premises: a) create a library, and b) do not destroy the lawn. For this reason, he decided that the two libraries in the shape of rhomboidal cages would float. The larger of the two offers poetry and history books and the other one children's books.

0839 In this observation lookout on the east coast of Norway, the design adheres to two requirements: a) respect for the existing pine trees: b) bringing nature closer to the visitor. The wooden pine structure is suspended by steel anchored on a concrete base, 98 feet from the highest point of the fjord.

0840 The sculptural character of the pieces designed by Vito Acconci is unquestionable. He worked during the 1970s as a sculptor and performance artist, which largely explains the dramatic qualities of his design. The interior of the sculptures display the skylights, which are open to the exterior.

0832

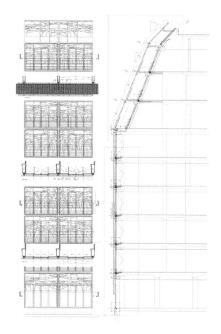

Exterior wall section detail and general wall section

0833

0834

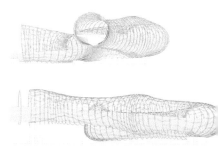

Renderings

0835

▽

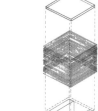

Interior structure of the cube

Support panels

Bundle of lighting cables

Base

0836

0837

Sketches

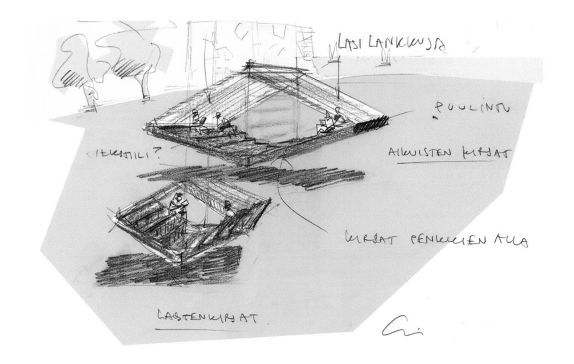

LASI LANKKUJA

PUULINTU

AIKUISTEN KIRJAT

TEKSTILI?

KIRJAT PENKKIEN ALLA

LASTENKIRJAT

tch

0840

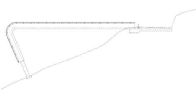

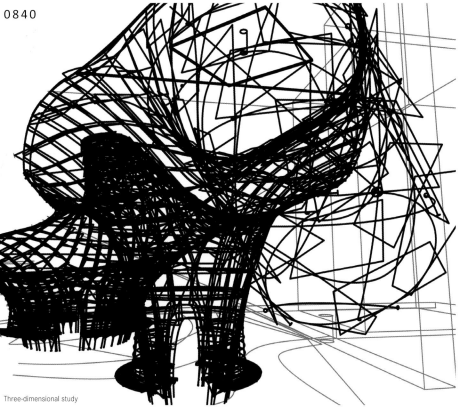

ation

Three-dimensional study

0841

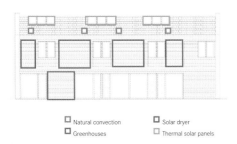

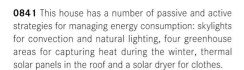

☐ Natural convection   ☐ Solar dryer

☐ Greenhouses   ☐ Thermal solar panels

Elevation with bioclimatic details

0842

0843

0844

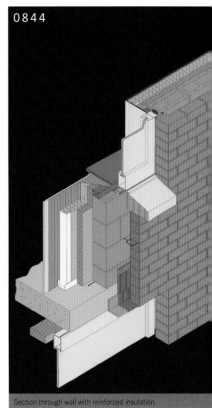

Section through wall with reinforced insulation

0841 This house has a number of passive and active strategies for managing energy consumption: skylights for convection and natural lighting, four greenhouse areas for capturing heat during the winter, thermal solar panels in the roof and a solar dryer for clothes.

0842 In the entrance area to the Dwight Way complex, in Berkeley, California, repurposed materials have been used, such as street signs for handrails and partitions, or the bulb from an old car headlight to light the garden beds.

0843 This house is not connected to the electrical grid. It is 100% self-sufficient thanks to the use of solar photovoltaic and thermal panels, as well as a wind energy generator, which generates 900 W at a speed of 29 mph.

0844 A cross-section diagram of the façade of the Solaire building shows variations to the brick wall used in a typical New York building. In this case, the insulation has been reinforced with rigid insulating panels and window seals both inside and outside.

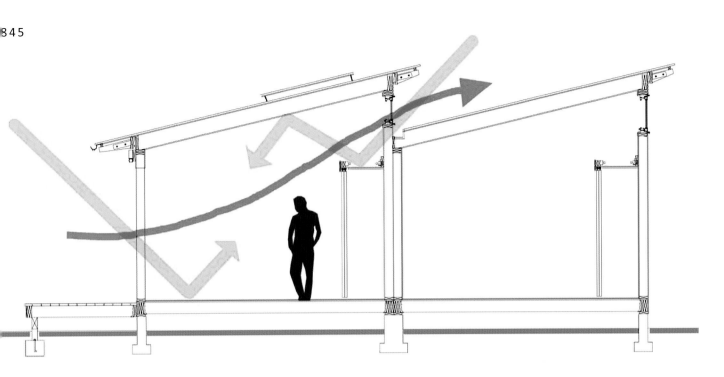

...climatic diagram

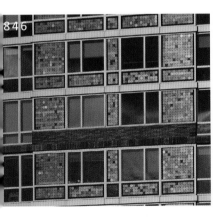

0847

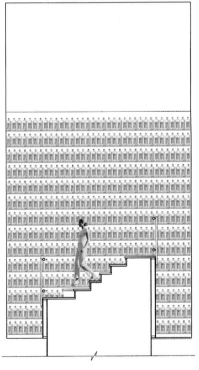

848

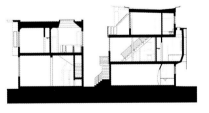

...orth-south section

Section through the tapestry with bottles area

0845 The interiors of this building have clerestory windows for cross-ventilation. The finishes are made from FSC certified wood and no toxic substances have been used to treat the surfaces: low-emission, volatile organic compound (VOC) paints have been used.

0846 The energy efficiency of this building should reduce energy consumption by 35% compared to a typical large building, and reduce peak power demand by 65%. Photovoltaic panels, producing 5% of the building's energy requirements, were placed on the façade.

0847 The bottles forming the wall sculpture of the F10 House act as thermal storage during the winter, as they absorb solar heat during the day and release it into the interior at night. During the winter a fan in the central area helps to pull warm air into the building through the clerestory window.

0848 The north-south section of the Dwight Way complex exemplifies the environmental objectives of this project: it uses recycled and/or repurposed materials, natural finishes and is highly energy efficient thanks to insulation and passive and active strategies.

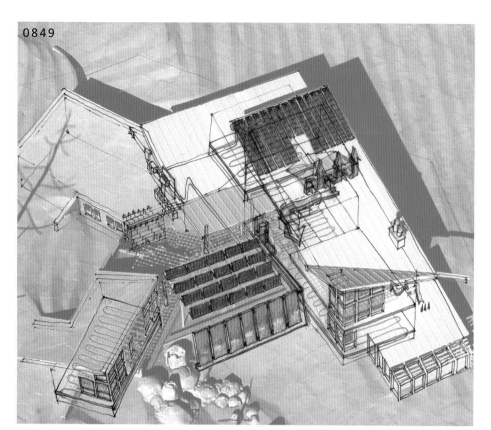

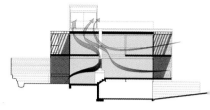

Bioclimatic diagram

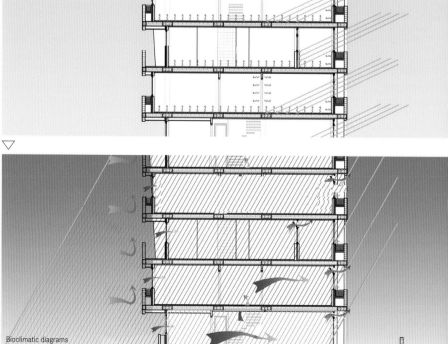

Bioclimatic diagrams

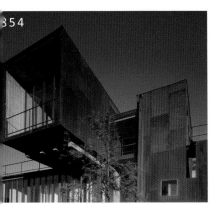

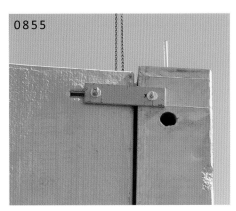

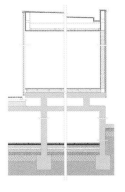

:tion

0856

857

0849 This residence in Eastern Sierra uses a series of passive and active strategies to achieve the highest possible energy self-sufficiency. The load bearing walls are made from straw bales with an earthen finish using local soil, with slatted cement-board siding.

0850 The Z6 House meets the requirements of the LEED Platinum Home category. Passive climate control strategies have been implemented, such as structuring the spaces into modules and having clerestory windows on the upper part, which creates a solar chimney effect and refreshes the environment.

0851 The 5.4.7 Arts Center produces 80 to 120% of the building's required energy through a combination of passive and active strategies. The building's double frame is made of FSC certified wood and glass, which increases the transfer of heat/cold by thermal mass.

0852 The bioclimatic section of this building indicates the methods for generating fresh air during the winter, such as cross-ventilation and the solar chimney effect caused by motorized skylights in the roof, which expel warm air into the dwelling.

0853 Two sections indicate the differences in the bioclimatic behavior of the building in two different seasons: in winter the heat accumulates in the floor during the day and radiates out at night. In summer, cross-ventilation allows warm air to be expelled, particularly on the southern side.

0854 Rusted steel panels make up the double façade that heats up this dwelling. In the internal air chamber, the air moves and cools the wooden interior wall. In this way, the home is protected from the warm northern climate of the Santiago Metropolitan Area in Chile where it is located.

0855 Prefabricated systems make dry assembly easier. In the Kyoto Home, in Torre Serona (Lérida), the prefabricated concrete elements are the enclosure walls, the structure of the pillars and beams, the interior and exterior panels, as well as the prefabricated stairs.

0856 In this home, cross-ventilation between the stone framework and wooden structure refreshes the interior in the summer. In the winter, when it snows and all the compartments are closed, the snow gathers on the framework and the house is thermally insulated from the outside, like a cave.

0857 The load bearing walls and the attic of this house in the Swiss town of Disentis were made from straw bales. The bales were tied together by hand using plastic tape. Once in place, the work paused so as to allow the material time to settle sufficiently.

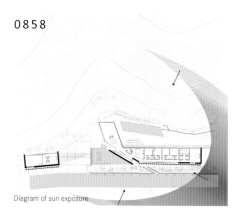

0858

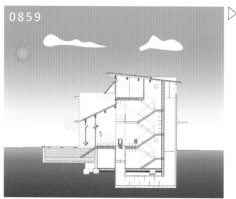

0859

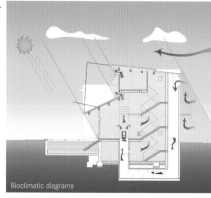

Diagram of sun exposure

Bioclimatic diagrams

0860

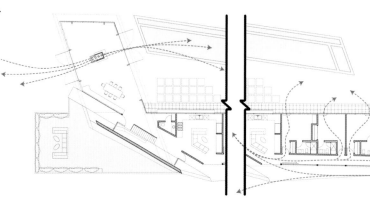

0858 One of the design premises for this building was to protect the space from the strong local solar radiation. The solar incidence diagram shows the blue glazed façades to the north and east. The façade is opaque on the sides that are most exposed to sunlight.

0859 Bioclimatic design, insulation and thermal inertia mean that this family home consumes 10% of the energy of a conventional home. The water in the swimming pool is heated by photovoltaic panels, which keep the water warm all year round.

0860 The diagram of cross-ventilation throughout this house shows the successful strategy that allows adequate ventilation in all rooms. This eliminates the need for air conditioning and reduces the house's energy consumption. The natural ventilation in the living room is especially effective.

0861 Inside this residence, the large metal beams of the structure that were recovered from the Big Dig project can be seen. The slabs supporting the roof are pieces of precast concrete that were previously a part of a demolished freeway ramp. In the stairwell, the double height creates a solar chimney effect.

0862 This laboratory from the 1950s was remodeled and reincarnated into an office block for WWF. Energetically self-sufficient with no CO_2 emissions, it uses natural materials such as clay, wood and reused bricks.

0861

0862

0863

Longitudinal section with bioclimatic diagram

0864

0865

0863 Dry assembly of this home, in only three days, reduced the total cost by 35%. The main structural components used in both the floor and roof are steel and concrete. These were salvaged from the demolition of the Big Dig macro project in Lexington, Massachusetts.

0864 In the Yesler community centre in Seattle, the strategies of opening up and ventilating the building have been combined to provide light and natural air conditioning. In this case, the building also benefits from a solar chimney effect in such a way that hot air is sucked up outwards.

0865 In areas of India, temperatures reach 113°F; this explains the design of the vaulted roofs with local clay walled up in concrete panels. The clay acts as an insulating layer, preventing heat from passing through. This natural material has a porcelain mosaic finish.

0866

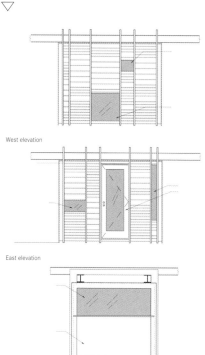

West elevation

East elevation

North elevation

Double glass or plywood and plywood sheet (0.5 inches)

0867

Exploded view

0868

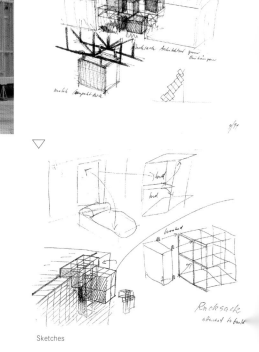

Sketches

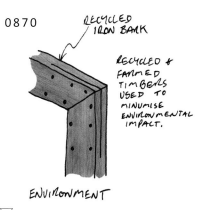

RECYCLED
IRON BANK

RECYCLED +
FARMED
TIMBERS
USED TO
MINIMISE
ENVIRONMENTAL
IMPACT.

ENVIRONMENT

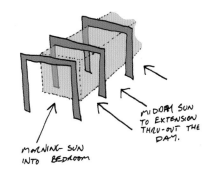

MIDDAY SUN
TO EXTENSION
THRU-OUT THE
DAY.

MORNING SUN
INTO BEDROOM

ection

Detailed illustrations of the structure

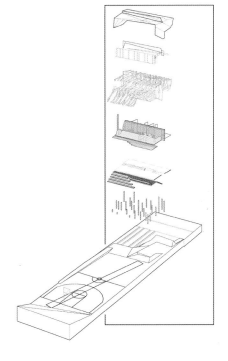

Exploded axonometric

0866 This cedar wood cabin was designed for a naturalist and bird-lover. For the front façade, double-glazed glass was used on the top half and 0.5 inch plywood boards on the bottom half. The rear façade is made from cedar and can be opened from the top half.

0867 The philosophy behind prefabricated construction is based on lowering costs and reducing the amount of leftover building material both in the factory and on site. The prefabricated units are efficiently transported by truck to the site, where they are assembled.

0868 The plans for the Rucksask House were based on the idea of an extension of the dwelling, in a cube shape which, like a parasite unit, was installed on two buildings in Leipzig and Cologne. It weighs 2,425 pounds and the plywood furniture inside is 100% foldable.

0869 Siegal has made the most of the industrial character of the site – The Brewery, a former beer production site converted into an artist's colony – to give this house a definite industrial feel. Four ISO freight containers and two cereal trailers were used to make it.

0870 The main environmental measures of the extension to this house on Essex Street are the use of sunlight, (morning sun in the bedroom and afternoon sun in the rest of the rooms) and the use of recycled materials in the wooden structure.

0871 In this studio-workshop, designed as a bird observatory for an environmental writer, there is a depression in the roof to collect rainwater for the fauna inside. The client wanted to hear the sound of running water and to be reminded of the area's hydrology.

0872 The construction of Burst* 003 was started in January 2005 and completed in December of that year, with the majority of the prefabricated elements already assembled by March. The main materials used in the construction were concrete, plywood, cedar wood, steel and glass.

0873 The prefabrication of elements in a factory and their on site assembly represents a significant savings in terms of raw materials and construction time. This house has been installed suspended above the ground to avoid the excess moisture, just a few yards from the beach.

0874 The original model of the EvolutiV House, exhibited at the Alpexpo in Grenoble and made entirely from chestnut wood, is formed from two ISO freight containers laid out at right angles, with one of the sides supported by a pile of logs.

0875 With the help of digital design, System Architects used the Burst* prototypes to create a complex geometry adapted to the relationship between the natural forces at the site and the schedule. In this way, they created a residence with low energy consumption.

0876 The use of ISO freight containers for residential dwellings requires slight compositional changes, as in the case of this house in Redondo Beach, California, which has glass façades with a balcony on the ground floor and clerestory windows on the upper floor.

0877 The whole extension of this residence makes use of sunlight thanks to folding and opening skylights. Built on an east-west axis, it is formed of a wooden structure covered in recycled 0.5-inch-thick steel.

0878 The combination of laminated steel profiles forms a prism shape on the southern façade. Its position on a downwards slope transforms the south façade into a sort of watchtower looking out over the Asturias countryside.

0879 This observation platform is comprised of symmetrical modules assembled randomly, according to the needs of the client. Once the modules are assembled, they form a platform of variable length, with a walkway across that has a glass handrail and a sloping bench.

0873

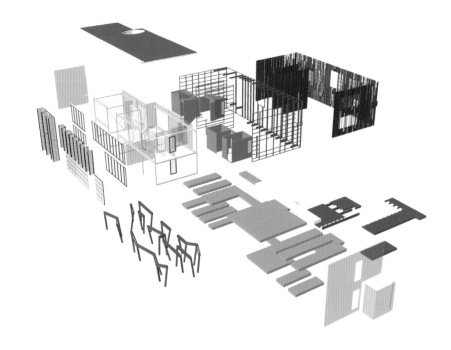

Exploded view of the prefabricated elements

0874

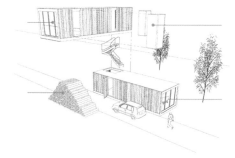

Exploded view

0876

0875

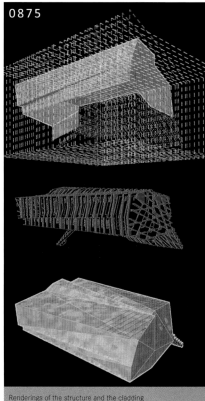

Renderings of the structure and the cladding

0877

rior perspective

879

spective of a standard module with furniture

0878

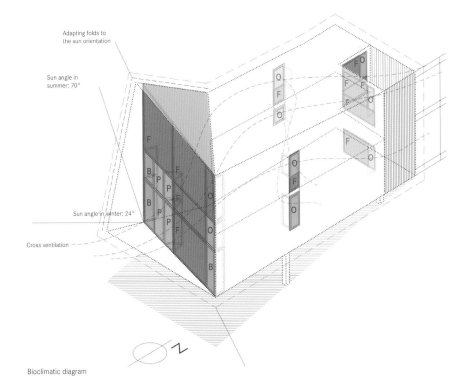

Adapting folds to
the sun orientation

Sun angle in
summer: 70°

Sun angle in winter: 24°

Cross ventilation

Bioclimatic diagram

0880 One of the premises of the X House project was the incorporation of an interior terrace, an essential element of Latin-American architecture, as well as exploring the possibilities of a prototype glass box in the temperate climate of Quito, where it is located.

0881 The clients wanted a simple, sustainable house and for this, the architects opted for a light wooden structure; the design promotes a reduced number of materials and the efficient use of these materials. The enclosure provides protection from the sun and rain, as well as allowing cross-ventilation.

0880

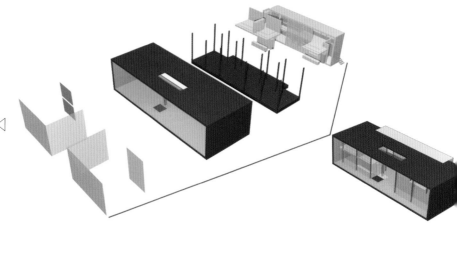

Exploded axonometric

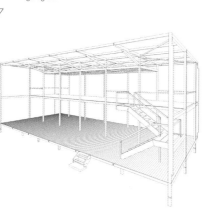

0881

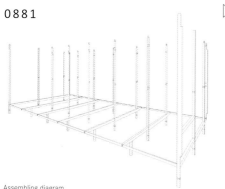

Assembling diagram

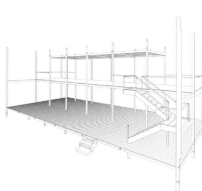

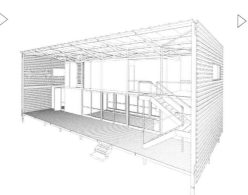

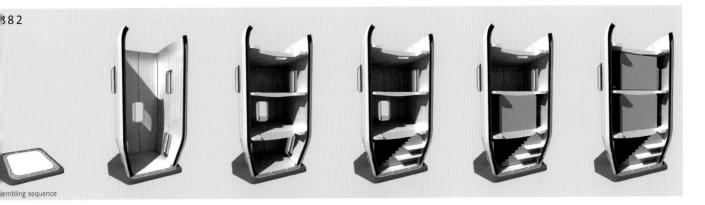

embling sequence

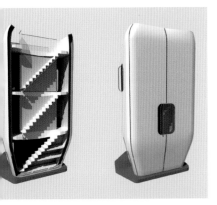

0883

884

0885

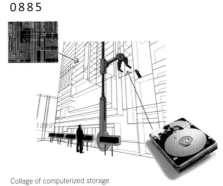

Collage of computerized storage

0886

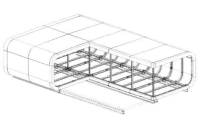

agram of the modular dwelling skeleton

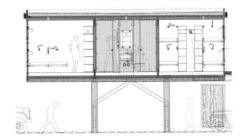

Longitudinal section of the apartment module

0882 Useful + Agreeable (U+A) is an architectural solution by NMDA, offering prefabricated houses to an emerging market of clients who value design and are looking for a style of residence to suit the products that surround them in their everyday life.

0883 The northern façade of this house is protected by a former space and a windbreaker blind. The double height has not been designed for reasons of space or composition, but rather as an essential bioclimatic tool for regulating the temperature of the house.

0884 Nomadhome is a patented system for flexible construction, involving joining units of 118 square feet together. It can be used for commercial or residential purposes. The units are interchangeable, expandable and can be disassembled whenever you like, in just two or three days.

0885 Andrew Maynard has created a computer library as a community cultural center and an intelligent space in which the borrowing and returning of books is controlled by an electronic system.

0886 This module-apartment is formed of a central unit housing the bathroom and American-style kitchen, two 65-square-foot bedrooms at opposing angles, and a 204.5-square-foot living area covered by a 21.5-square-foot gallery. The ground floor, which is open thanks to the large projection of the structure, serves as a parking space.

0887

0888

0889

0890

0887 Plastic relief flooring is a highly recommended solution for especially slippery surfaces that need maximum safety, such as the submerged area around the edge of the pool.

0888 It is becoming increasingly common for swimming pools to look out, apparently without barriers, over the sea and the horizon at the far edge of a plot of land. This is a spectacular decorative effect. The pool in the image also has a series of submerged bar stools and a "wet bar".

0889 The ceramic floor tiles surrounding this pool are crowned with a tiled strip, and at the very edge, some partially submerged wooden strips that help to prevent slipping also serve as seating.

0890 The curved series of concrete bollards running from one side to the other across this swimming pool is not supposed to be a pathway, but to demarcate the spaces between areas of varying depths.

0891 The steps leading to this swimming pool have been ever so carefully designed. The small mosaic tiles adapt perfectly to the winding curves of the steps, while the change in color at the edge means that the edge of the step can be seen from out of the water.

0892 A narrow swimming pool had to be designed to fit into this small garden. With the same width as a competition pool, it is just sufficient for swimming laps. The floor tiling, in an elegant cream-colored marble, transforms the environment into an oasis of calm.

0893 It is an unusual layout when the steps to the pool are installed in one corner. In this case, the concentric steps are laid out in graduated arcs, with a central handrail to help people get in and out.

0894 Carefully chosen ceramic glazed and mosaic tiles give this indoor pool an extremely elegant look, somewhere between modern and classical. This, combined with traditional decorative elements such as the amphorae, creates a spectacular effect.

0895 The internal wall of this pool seems to be a curved shape, and this effect is created very simply: by applying a layer of white plastic paint to the cement wall. Under the water, it appears raised, due to an optical illusion similar to that of a magnifying glass.

0896 To ensure sufficient depth and user comfort, the ground surrounding the pool was raised up a couple of steps in relation to the rest of the floor, so that it rests on a plinth which helps it to stand out.

0897 This very small-sized pool is a good example of combining the blue tones of water with a deck area made of wood, a material which also stands out as being extraordinarily water-resistant when treated with the appropriate products.

0898 In this pool, the kiddies' area is several inches higher than the surface of the water of the rest of the construction. The idea is to make it easier to keep an eye on this space, and to achieve an attractive multi-layer effect landscape.

0899 This pool was designed so that, when full, there is hardly any difference between the surface of the water and the start of the edge, creating a lovely effect that increases the angle between the two types of flooring.

0900 This pool, with a more classic layout, has a rugged stone flooring surrounding it, and a raised edge that stops the water from getting dirty and acts as a barrier to prevent people from slipping over.

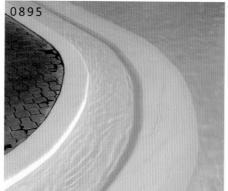

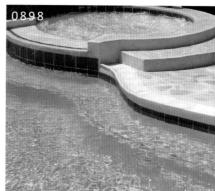

0901 This spectacular indoor swimming pool is remarkable because it has been built on the ground floor of an old house, making use of the vaulted shape of the ceiling and the space between the pillars that support the upper floor.

0902 The use of differently colored ceramic glazed tiles is a very simple and economical way to add a decorative element to the bottom of a swimming pool. There are endless possibilities of shapes, and color combinations.

0903 A low wall covered in the same blue ceramic glazed tiles as on the bottom, divides this pool into a bathing area and an area which has talassotherapy water jets. This increases enjoyment of the pool, as it prevents too much water being removed from it.

0904 The final stretch of this pool's wall, immediately before the edge, is decorated with a mosaic design inspired by the Ancient Greek patterns. The combination of these darker blue spirals with the ceramic glazed tiles on the bottom of the pool is spectacular.

0905 The varying tones of blue in the tiles covering the wall combine perfectly not only with the pool tiling, but also with the checkerboard paving surrounding it.

0906 In this case it is the pool's sun deck that appears to stretch out into the abyss, since there are no visible walls separating it from the surrounding landscape. This optical illusion results in a minimalist garden design.

0907 The edges of this indoor pool gradually flow upwards, to enable access to the Jacuzzi. The great height of the glass pavilion allowed for this difference in levels, transforming the site into a complete home spa.

906

907

0908

0909

0910

0912

General plan

0911

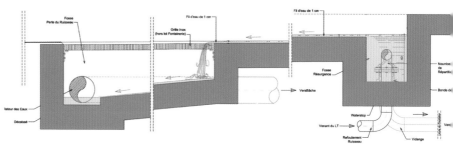

Section through the water mechanism system

913

914

915

0916

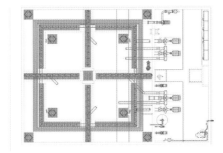

Detailed plan of the water intake

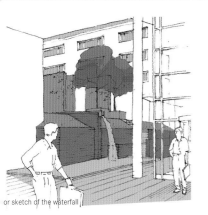

or sketch of the waterfall

Section through the water outlet

0908 In the Water Park in Le Blanc-Mesnil, the large central lake appears and disappears in accordance with the time of year. In summer, the plaza becomes a shallow urban pool, an oasis to escape the heat. The vegetation that surrounds the space is helophyte, common to wetland.

0909 In this project, it was faulty piping that led to the architect's idea of allowing rainwater to flow in full view on the surface of the location. The piping was replaced with a stone channel leading to a galvanized steel scupper and a cement wall that serves as a dam.

0910 For this public area, low walls and a roof of recovered granite block were built. The plot that was previously occupied by a mansion has become a park with seats, balance bars and an interactive fountain molded from recovered material.

0911 The Water Park project in Le Blanc-Mesnil requires rooms where the mechanics necessary to carry out the effects of the park are housed. The hydraulic circuit is closed, in such a way that the water is continuously recycled. A filtration system maintains the water at a certain health standard.

0912 This seasonal installation was carried out in Lausanne. The team of landscape architects decided to combine the characteristics of the site — sloping lands and industrial environment — to create a garden with industrial connotations. The "staircase" was made from four containers filled with gravel, water and water lilies.

0913 These details are from the distribution project of a series of public plazas, located in Frederiksberg, near Copenhagen. The overcast climate of the area and the presence of water established the design guidelines. The water and the night-time lighting are combined together to represent spectral areas with mist and the sounds of birds, frogs and owls.

0914 This fountain is in La Place du Nombre d'Or in Montpellier, designed by Ricardo Bofill. Jean Max Llorca, winner of the contest to design a fountain in this plaza, was inspired by the geometry of the golden ratio, which represents the divine proportion and has mystic connotations.

0915 Water represents one of the main elements of the gardens of the IBM office complex in Amsterdam. This is present in the ponds of the exterior boundary of the complex on the hill of the central patio, where the canal flows down from the north façade to the south and forms the resulting waterfall.

0916 Designed in accordance with the "golden ratio", the fountain forms a pattern of squares and triangles as the water falls vertically. At times, pyramids are formed, other rivers or light mist. The diagram shows the system of how the water enters and exits.

0917 For the Tanner Springs Park, Atelier Dreiseitl is planning a space that memorializes 200 years of the industrial past of this area in Portland. The site is characterized by the vegetation and the streams that stem from the pond.

0918 In the Queens Botanical Gardens in New York, Atelier Dreiseitl seeks to prick the conscience of visitors, through the design of storage systems and the reuse of rainwater. The diagram shows the surface-run off water collection system.

0919 This park located in northern Denmark has been designed with children in mind. The enclave is formed by a series of platforms on a gravel surface. Some of the platforms have vegetation, while in others, the concave platforms retain water in puddles when it rains. The fountains function throughout week.

0920 Although water does not physically feature, this 344-square-foot seasonal installation on the roof of a downtown building in Montreal is totally inspired by this liquid. The circles in this installation represent water droplets and underline conscientious urban use of rain water.

0921 The rebuilding of the natural habitat and the construction of the ornithology museum justify the design of small vegetated islands in the middle of an artificial lake that allows birds to rest during their migratory transit. There are also walkways to allow observation of the birds without disturbing them.

0922 This fountain is located in a park on the riverbank of the Lake Constance, marked with references to the history and culture of Kreuzlingen. With a sombre design focused on elongated features, the landscape architect tries to bring to mind the erosion of the canals around the city.

0923 This space in Campinas, Brazil that dates to the end of the 21st century was extremely deteriorated. SInce being renovated, it boasts a row of trees that give shade, a row of jets, some ponds and stone benches. The jets are the most dynamic element of a rather functional design.

0924 The water determines the character of the different areas of this park in the shape of springs, waterfalls, jets, brooks or ponds. In this case, an existing infrastructure has been used for this design: the purifier Los Tanques-Morrorrico in Bucaramanga, Colombia, represents the waterfall.

0925 This jet is one of the 15 that, with total simplicity, represents the element water in the Cufar plaza in Jesenice, Slovenia. The objective of the design was to create an open space. The ground, paved as if it were a crosswalk, is surrounded by a school, library, theatre, a cinema and several bars.

0918

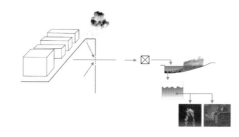

Water runoff collection scheme

0919

0922

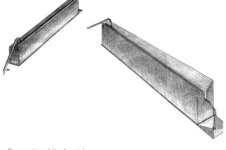

Perspective of the fountain

0924

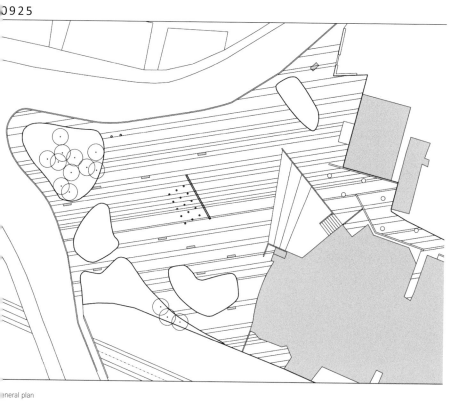

0925

general plan

0926

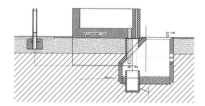

Section through the area of water outlet

0927

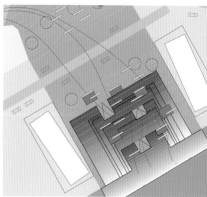

0928

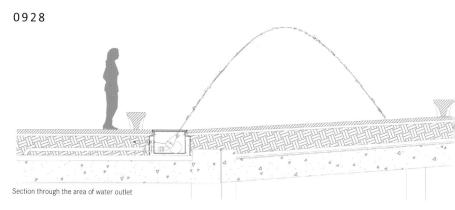

Section through the area of water outlet

0929

Cross section

0926 This detail shows how the fountain on this patio of the primary school in Hallau, Switzerland works, which creates an artificial brook. The thread of water that feeds the imagination of the students flows between the north part of the complex and the fountain situated in the south.

0927 This plaza is next to the main jetty in Thisted, Denmark. It is made from square concrete slabs that float on a pond with different inclined steps. The design encourages the close relationship between this locality and the sea, as if it were this that bathed its shores.

0928 The system of fountains in the new Barcelona Fair consists of a series of jets located in small plazas of undulating elements, designed by JML Arquitectura del Agua. The presence of water dynamizes a geometric environment.

0929 This green area gains space from an area formerly occupied by houses in Enschede, The Netherlands, that were destroyed by the explosion of a nearby firecracker factory. The design encourages the presence of water directed by canals of varying width (up to 23 feet), in which a series of asymmetric stone slabs serve to cross from one side to the other.

0930 This garden is in a home in Miami. The shallow pond is the prevalent feature of this part of the garden facing south. The water comes from the waterfall that rises from the vertical fissure in the wall. The pond is made from rectangular stone slabs and contains aquatic species.

0931 This small garden that is reminiscencent of southeast Asia has a natural stone wall as the main element, from which water falls in the form of a waterfall. Before coming to rest in a small pond decorated with aquatic species and stone slabs, the water collides against a corbel.

0932 This rectangular and elongated pond is located in one of the corners of the property. The layer of water serves as a simple restrained and zen counterpoint to a garden where a paved island is the prevalent feature, and where outdoor tables and chairs are located. The design is finished off with trees and gravel on the majority of the land.

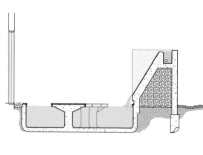

Section through the pond and the waterfall

0931

0932

0933

0934

0935

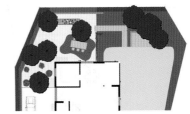
General plan of the garden with the pond

Diagram of a section through the oval ring

0933 In this project, the architect sought to capture the reflections of the water. Using its aerodynamic flow through a polished black granite surface area, the architect has managed to reflect the images that surround the fountain. Under the tranquil mirror that forms part of the top half of the fountain, water falls quietly and raptly.

0934 The monument in memory of the Princess of Wales, erected in 2004 in London is made up of an oval ring of De Lank granite, from the quarry located near Cornwall, along which water is constantly pumped in two directions from a fountain located on the upper part of the oval perimeter.

0935 This park in Singapore forms part of the One-North master plan by Zaha Hadid in the city's technology district. West 8 designed the parkland among mixed-use buildings. Amid the green area, water falls over a vertical wall. At night, the space is decorated with small LED spotlights.

0936 The façade of this spectacular building by Kengo Kuma is formed by a series of wide wooden strips that hide a set of long planter boxes. The wood alternates with a growing band of vegetation to become the building's main decorative feature.

0937 The architects of this residential complex overcame the scarcity of space available for gardens with a relatively simple solution: they covered most of the façades with ivy and vines that climb from ground-level garden beds.

0938 Different species of hardy climbing plants and heather that resist low temperatures form a spectacular skin for the façade of this building. The metal window jambs are inserted into the vegetation layer without visible fastenings.

0939 The glass façades of this restaurant have a spectacular screen, created by the artist Aude Franjou, that imitates the form of dried up trees, but in reality has been made from twine and flax.

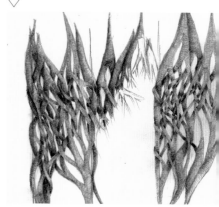

0940 The planted façade in the atrium of this office block, apart from being pleasing to the eye, provides a passive climate control system that consumes no energy at all. The plants refresh the air during the summer and regulate changes in temperature during the winter.

0941 To accomodate the pronounced slope upon which the house is built, the mountain was incorporated as a retaining wall. The rock can be seen in the bathroom on the lower floor, and in the living room located in the entrance area on the upper floor.

0942 Plantwall, a vertical planted element, located in a stairwell and designed by Green Fortune, purifies the air and humidifies the home environment. Plant fertilizer is distributed within the four-layered textile membrane of the wall by drip-feed watering.

0943 The use of the natural rock as an enclosure wall is evident from outside and inside the house, particularly in areas such as the bathroom and bedroom. The architect has made the most of this setting in the rugged Costa Brava so as to have the best views of the sea.

0944

▷

0945

0946

0947

0948

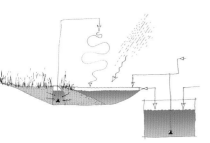

Schematic design of the water concept

Sketch with species distribution

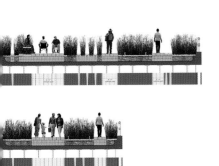

Sections

0944 Living Wall systems combine Autocad production techniques with live elements such as plants. These purify the air and provide acoustic and thermal insulation. Carefully selected plants, drip irrigation and daylighting mean they are adaptable to different conditions.

0945 The design of the headquarters of the construction developer Vivico has clear lines and organic attributes. In the foyer the illusion/allusion of the vertical garden (backlit panels in the backdrop) becomes a reality with the parterre below the stairwell.

0946 This office complex occupies a floor with two parallelogram-shaped levels around a central, richly landscaped courtyard of 107,639 square feet. The outer perimeter of the complex is formed by a mesh structure with wisteria and vines forming a vertical garden.

0947 This detail shows a big mossy stone wall that, like a backbone, runs through the longitudinal elevation, creating a dividing line between the living areas to the west, and the bathrooms and children's bedrooms to the east. The hearth is lined with the same stone.

0948 This natural pool combines the pleasure of swimming and the benefits of a water garden. The water covers an area of 32.8 × 9.84 feet, including the waterfall between stones and the area with aquatic plants, which apart from being decorative also serve as a water cleansing biotope.

0949 This project has recovered former brownfield sites in Portland for its citizens. Located near the Willamette River, the park has a small pond that is cleansed by means of a biotope. The water level is periodically regulated and surplus water is stored in a cistern tank.

0950 Patrick Blanc, the famous botanist specializing in vertical gardens, conceived the idea behind these planted walls that are suspended on a galvanized steel structure with a layer of synthetic felt that incorporates the drip irrigation. In this case, the distribution of species can be observed.

0951 The High Line is a raised rail line that was built in the 1930s. It was taken out of service in 1980, and in 2002 the City of New York gave the green light to a project to convert it into a public space. The program, which is a synthesis between ecology and urbanism, will allow citizens to stroll over the old railway track.

0952

0952 The universal love of climbing trees makes this tree house an ideal play space for children and a relaxing area for adults. In the rest room, two of the trees that support the structure appear between cushions, as if they were as a guest that continually reminds us of the reason behind the construction.

0953 The abundance of natural pools in central European countries creates visions like this residence in Neustadt, Germany, where a waterfall leads down to a pond-pool, which is converted into a wild element, despite its location in a built-up area.

0954 The main block of this home facing the coast is left deliberately unpolished. As a counterpoint, the architect decided to provide two more organic elements: a wall made from stone and a roof made from randomly-positioned stones.

0955 For this small house located in Kobe, Japan, the architect opted to highlight natural rather than urban elements. This is a style that is typical of Japanese architecture, where natural elements on the inside and outside of the home have a special presence.

0956 This rectangular-shaped home has a Japanese-style bamboo garden in its back lawn that allows the user to integrate nature into the actual architectural volume. From the living room on the first floor it can be better appreciated how this fast-growing plant becomes another element of the home.

0957 For this shop in Seoul, Mass Studies seeks to create a live façade as if it were a synthesis of interior and exterior nature and objects. The exterior finish is covered with a geotextile layer with evergreen species such as lichens, moss and seaweed.

0958 The interior design of this Slovakian restaurant has an old-fashioned décor. The stone walls are the predominant feature along with the wood, copper and the homemade glass. Clients can rest on comfortable skin rugs, surrounded by lumps of rocks and river pebbles.

0959 This rock is located at the entrance to a village. This project, which was more reconstruction than remodel, used an old farmhouse located between a river and a eucalyptus forest as a starting point. The original stone walls were reused and conserved this irrefutable example of fusion between the house and local geology.

Tree house illustration

0953

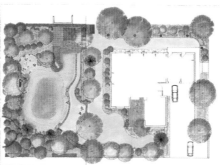

Floor plan

0954

0955

0956

0957

0958

0959

0960

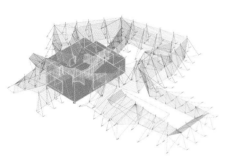

Diagram

0961

Project rendering

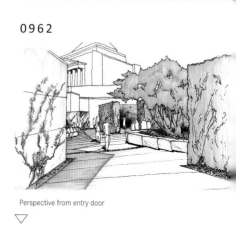

0962

Perspective from entry door

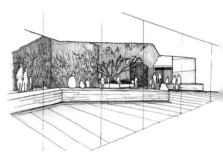

Perspective from multipurpose room

Design development collage

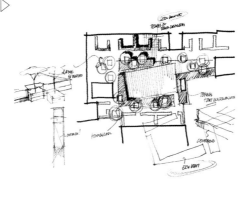

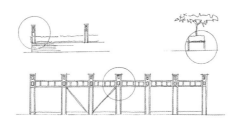

Development sketches

0960 This rural house has a 21,500-square-foot garden. Trees have been planted and covered over with polypropylene plastic mesh, creating a sort of maze between the branches. It is hoped that in five years, the house and garden will blend in with the environment.

0961 This former industrial yard has been converted into a green space for housing and offices. A diagonal asphalted walkway connects the yard entrance area with the offices. This is a linear structure around which the garden and the existing furniture is arranged.

0962 This is the garden of the visitors' center of the First World War Memorial in Melbourne, Australia. Its central design feature is the olive tree in the center of the garden, which is a symbol of peace. Areas set aside for contemplation are enclosed by hedges of laurel and oak.

0963 Water is the central element in this garden located in the central courtyard of the new IBM offices in Amsterdam. On the landscaped slopes of the central courtyard there is a system of gradients that move the water to the lowest level, with a waterfall near the pathway that enters the site.

0964 This garden, created as part of the rehabilitation project of the Palais du Tokyo in Paris, has brought back to life a space that had been abandoned for many years. Due to the fact that it is narrow and shaded, tropical species were planted that can adapt to humidity and colonization.

0965 This garden is located in the central courtyard of a residential complex built over the ground floor of commercial premises. Its main features consist of a lighting system with stainless steel towers, mesh pergolas, and exposed brick masonry in the planters and façades.

0966

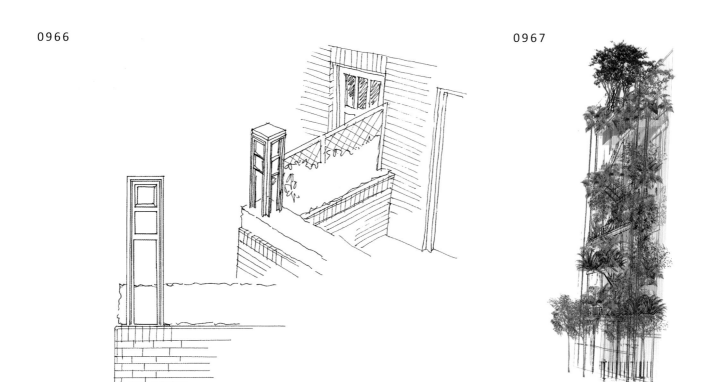

Sketch of raised garden bed

0967

Color rendering

0968

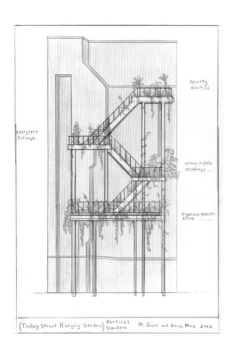

Preliminary sketch

0969

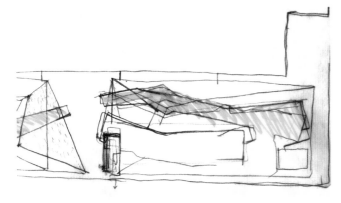

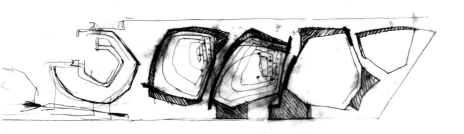

rden roof sketches

971

0972

0966 The axonometrics of the lit towers, and their plan, layout and section underline the geometrical and rational forms of this design. The towers are placed in the planters which makes them seem to have been born out of the shrubs themselves.

0967 In this project, the Scottish architects GROSS. MAX and the American artist Mark Dion envisioned a vertical garden climbing the emergency staircase on the façade of a building. Drip irrigation waters the vegetation, which consists of both native and exotic plants, and is dominated by an ailanthus.

0968 The vegetation in this street hanging garden is layered with quick growing species at the base, ruderal plants in the middle together with evergreen species, and a group of exotic species at the top of the staircase, next to a deciduous ailanthus of Asian origin that can reach 148 feet in height.

0969 A total of 16 courtyards of similar sizes and different shapes alternate throughout this office complex. The main elements of these designs are stone, wood and a diverse selection of plants, hedges, and, to a lesser extent, trees.

0970 These sketches are from the courtyard landscape design for the Macallen building, located above an underground garage. The aim was to reduce the greenhouse effect in Boston, and collect rainwater in a tank located between the planting bed and the garage foundations.

0971 The materials used in this small garden in Brazil are granite, gravel, pebbles, and wood, as well as plant species such as *Ophiopogon japonicus* and *Phyllostachys heteroclytaforma*. The result is a space with geometric shapes of alternating textures and colors.

0972 Due to the narrow proportions of the lot of this house in Kyoto and its proximity to roads, this garden is a sound-proofing element and a private landscape towards which the rooms of the house are oriented. It acts as a visual oasis in an asphalt landscape.

0973

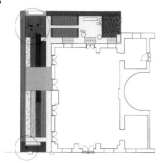

General plan

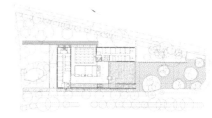

0974

General plan

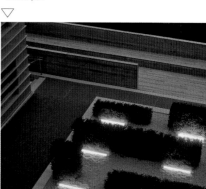

0973 This yard is a place for leisure and gardening, and is an extension of the interior living spaces. Due to its small size, it is very compartmentalized. Ornamental species are placed in front of the living room, while the vegetable garden is located in front of the kitchen next to a rest area.

0974 Railroads are the inspiration behind this garden created for the Berlin Federal Railroad Department. There are linear parterres of illuminated shrubs between the buildings and the wooden walkway leading from the offices to the wooded area.

0975

Preliminary studies

0975 This garden, broken down at compositional level, was the result of a restoration of the roof of a former distillery. It features large terraces where bamboo is the connecting element. Wood and natural stone paving is combined with mobile planters and ponds.

0976 A slight ramp with gravel, surrounded by a lawn, bushes, four fruit trees and two rows of daffodils at both ends represents the garden at the entrance to this home. The rear garden is a closed, minimalist and contemplative patio surrounded by cement walls.

0977 The central feature in the garden is a pond with a central platform that is accessed from the living area via a concrete walkway. A table and bench on the platform create a dining space among calming waters.

0978 The design of this garden complements the modern and functional character of this residence. In order to gain more privacy, a relaxed and sculptural interior landscape was creating using a variety of vegetation. The diagram shows the garden with granite sculptures placed between deciduous trees.

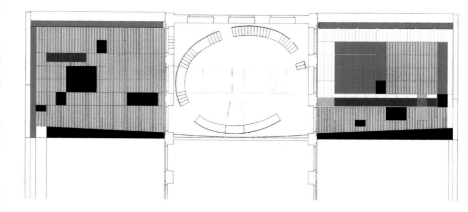

General plan

0976

0977

0978

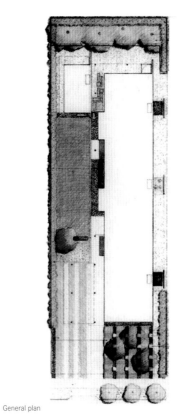

General plan

0979

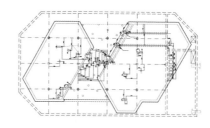

Floor plan

0979 Divided into two pool spaces, this urban fountain serves to cool the park in months of high temperatures. With the idea that it can practically serve as a water park, movement between the two pools is over a deck of wooden slats which stops the water from stagnating and prevents the possibility of people slipping.

0980 The appeal of this private patio located between the buildings of a residential complex is its minimalist, almost Zen-like nature. Importance has been given to the color of the paving, which is embellished by extremely simple urban furniture featuring unadorned, backless benches.

0981 The structure of metal pillars providing shade to this area of a public square is a substitute for vegetation. In fact, its color scheme and the tree shapes formed by the slats are an indication of this function.

0982 The space between the units in this complex is connected by gray dolomite stone slabs covering the ground. This remarkable design has irregular shaped slabs in a continuous shape, with green seams of various widths covering the remaining areas.

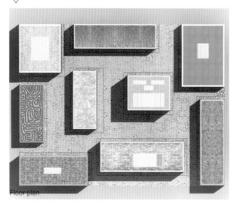

Floor plan

983

ches

984

0985

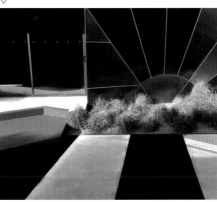

0983 This garden is located in the center of a typical communal patio and is surrounded on all four sides by apartment blocks. The space immerses the residents in ever-changing environments, since the chosen vegetation provides an all-round sensory experience of sight, sound and taste.

0984 The light roof floating over the undulating ground is made up of Brazilian walnut wood and aluminum panels. Abundant vegetation has been planted to prevent people seeing directly into the ground floor windows.

0985 This landscaping project combines sophisticated shapes, varying surfaces and the use of different color schemes. The black and white striped cement and asphalt paving transforms, at the edges, into a pattern of polygons in gray and white tones, with the exception of the blue steps.

0986 The colored patterns of the paving is used to organize and structure the different scheduled activities and uses into different areas. A variety of trees and a selection of rounded rocks mark out pathways across the paving and also serve as seating areas.

0987 Various green seats were installed in the interior patio of this residential development, to be used as minimalist gazebos. The rest of the design comprises a simple three-way wooden platform, a graveled area for each entrance and random green areas.

0988 The client wished to create a few areas where employees could enjoy nature and meet up to have a chat during breaks from work. Small stainless steel bridges, which resemble the materials of the façade, allow people to cross the canal which opens out into an irregular-shaped pond. The outdoor terrace is paved with gray sandstone slabs.

0989 In the Forest Gallery, a piece of rainforest has been created in the mountains close to Melbourne. The space is designed as a living sculpture formed of vegetation, natural and man-made materials and digital technology. Visitors can even access a space/installation that explores the human effect on this environment.

0990 One of the remarkable features of this square is its smooth profile, which is emphasized by the checkerboard paving of stone and aluminum grills. The trees have a uniform layout, so that this feature is accentuated.

0991 The lit walls and projections in this square create and demarcate areas for meeting or practicing various activities. Various architectural resources were used, such as marquees, illuminated walls and built-in furniture, circular benches and green hedged walls.

0992 The centre of the square features jets of water which spurt directly out of the asphalt and create different displays that can be remotely controlled. The square can change at any moment: the white lines can be painted different colors. The surface looks like an enormous crosswalk.

0993 This wide central square, located in the Royal Docks in London, is composed of a level area of lawn and an area with interactive fountains. Steel, natural stone, concrete and wood were used in the construction.

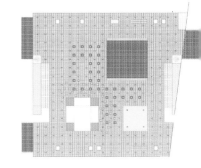

Floor plan

92

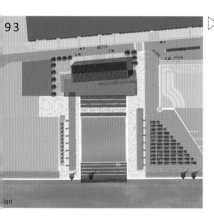

93

lan

0994

0995

0996

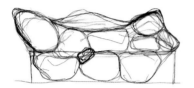

Sketch and section

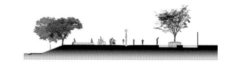
Side elevation and section

0994 This garden is constructed around a pool of water surrounded by a wooden walkway. Various three-dimensional metallic shapes rest delicately on a bed of mint plants. These structures, made from a mesh of netting and wire wool, resemble large cushions.

0995 The square was intended as a space that can be crossed in all directions and its design was based on parallel guiding principles that mirror the few elements present: water, vegetation and seating. These three functional lines interrupt the continuous surface of the ground, which is paved with gray stone slabs.

0996 The architect Carlos Martínez and the artist Pipilotti Rist have transformed a monotonous crossroads into an urban living area featuring intensely red-colored rubber paving. The carpeting extends out as far as the edge of the buildings.

0997 Various designs have been used on the strips that cover and flow over the entire park, which is located in an urban environment: solid brick, areas with brick and grass, or completely turfed areas.

0997

0998 This square's most remarkable feature is the golden metallic canopy supported by bronze poles that resemble old-fashioned gardening sticks. The rest of the square is made up of areas with tables for playing games, an amphitheater and thee water spaces for visitors to interact with.

0999 Water is an ever-present element in the design of this space; the jets of water were laid out so as to reflect the geometry of the architecture. These create controlled volumes of water and are inserted between the benches, whose lines blend with the shapes.

1,000 The Perth Memorial Garden in Australia was made with from sandstone, granite and steel. It highlights the Australian culture and landscape using images of indigenous flora and fauna, represented in the steel walls.

999

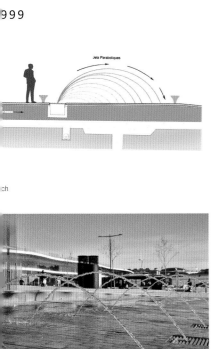

1,000

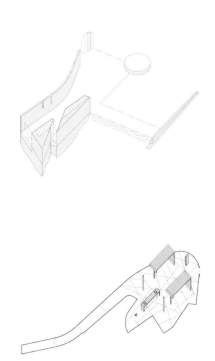

Axonometric projections

0001
© Hannu Liivaar/Dreamstime.com
0002
© Kai Zhang/Dreamstime.com
0003
© Ilja Masik/Dreamstime.com
0004, 0294
© Pavel Losevsky/Dreamstime.com
0005
© Ene/Dreamstime.com
0006
© Jian Zhang/Dreamstime.com
0007
Miró Rivera Architects
www.mirorivera.com
© Paul Finkel/Piston Design
0008, 0132, 0423, 0565
Víctor Cañas, Joan Roca/Aquart
www.victor.canas.co.cr
www.aquart.net
© Jordi Miralles
0009
Tadao Ando
www.tadao-ando.com
© Mitsuo Matsuoka
0010, 0741
Renzo Piano Building Workshop
www.rpbw.com
© Ishida Shunji (0010)
0011
© Deborah Benbrook/Dreamstime.com
0012
© Simon Schmidt/Dreamstime.com
0013
© Ana Vasileva/Dreamstime.com
0014
Alberto Campo Baeza
www.campobaeza.com
© Hisao Suzuki
0015
Daniel Bonilla Arquitectos
www.daniel-bonilla.com
© Daniel Bonilla Arquitectos
0016
© Oleg Fedorenko/Dreamstime.com
0017, 0035, 0062, 0065, 0168, 0323, 0936
Kengo Kuma & Associates
www.kkaa.co.jp
© Mitsumasa Fujitsuka (0017, 0035, 0323, 0936)
© Daici Ano (0062, 0065, 0168)
0018, 0037, 0071, 0095, 0096, 0379, 0493
Despang Architekten
www.despangarchitekten.de
© Despang Architekten
0019, 0397, 0407, 0759
123DV architectuur & consult bv
www.123dv.nl
© 123DV architectuur & consult bv (0397)
© Christiaan de Bruijne, Constantin Meyer (0019, 0407, 0759)
0020, 0022, 0121, 0174
Archteam
www.archteam.cz
© Ester Havlová
0021, 0033, 0304, 0385
Jensen & Skodvin Arkitektkontor
www.jsa.no
© Jensen & Skodvin Arkitektkontor
0022, (0020)
0023, 0212, 0495, 0691
Estudio Lamela Arquitectos, Richard Rogers Partnership
www.lamela.com
www.richardrogers.co.uk
© Manuel Renau

0024, 0025
© Justin Sailor/Dreamstime.com
0025, (0024)
0026
Ari Bungers/LAB Arkkitehdit Oy
www.lab-arkkitehdit.fi
© Ari Bungers/LAB Arkkitehdit Oy
0027
Paolo Cesaretti
www.paolocesaretti.it
© Paolo Cesaretti
0028
Mattinson Associates
www.mattinsonassociates.com
© Carlos Dominguez, Mattinson Associates
0029
Driendl Architects
www.driendl.at
© Driendl Architects
0030
Alla Kazovsky Architects
nneka@taylor-pr.com
© Alla Kazovsky Architects, Josh Perrin
0031
Eric Owen Moss Architects
www.ericowenmoss.com
© Tom Bonner
0032, 0034, 0175, 0430, 0559
Tham & Videgård Hansson Arkitekter
www.tvh.se
© Åke E:son Lindman
0033, (0021)
0034, (0032)
0035, (0017)
0036, 0324
Berger + Parkinnen Architekten
www.berger-parkkinen.com
© Berger + Parkinnen Architekten
0037, (0018)
0038, 0081, 0145, 0239, 0240, 0680, 0723, 0980
Camezind Evolution
www.camenzindevolution.com
© Camezind Evolution
0039, 0562
Foreign Office Architecture
www.f-o-a.net
© Francisco Andeyro García, Alejandro García González (0562)
© Kim Jae-Kyung (0039)
0040, 0043, 0046, 0136, 0140
Andreas Fuhrimann Gabrielle Hächler Architekten
www.afgh.ch
© Fuhrimann Hächler (0040)
© Valentin Jeck (0043, 0046, 0136, 0140)
0041
JKMM Architects
www.jkmm.fi
© Arno de la Chapelle, Jussi Tiainen, Kimmo Räisänen
0042, 0301
Mount Fuji Architects Studio
www14.plala.or.jp/mfas/fuji.htm
© Mount Fuji Architects Studio
0043, (0040)
0044, 0103, 0376
GAD-Global Architectural Development
www.gadarchitecture.com
© Ali Bekman (0044)
© Ali Bekman, Ozlem Ercil (0103, 0376)
0045
Martín Gomez Arquitectos
www.martingomezarquitectos.com
© Daniela Mac Adden
0046, (0040)

0047, 0150, 0372
Paul Morgan Architects
www.paulmorganarchitects.com
© Peter Bennetts (0047)
© John Gollings (0150, 0372)
0048, 0151
SKAARA Arkitekter AS
www.skaara.no
© Frank Tolpinrud
© Espen Grønli
0049
BIG – Bjarke Ingels Group
JDS – Julien de Smedt Architects
www.big.dk
www.jdsarchitects.com
© BIG – Bjarke Ingels Group
0050
Juan Pablo Corvalán/Supersudaka
www.supersudaka.cl
© Supersudaka.com
0051
Casagrande Laboratory
www.clab.fi
© Casagrande Laboratory
0052
Paul Bernier Architecte
www.paulbernier.com
© Paul Bernier, Vittorio Viera
0053, 0054, 0057, 0058
Cazú Zegers AIRA Arquitectos
www.cazuzegers.cl
© Guy Wenborne (0053, 0054)
© Juan Purcell, Guy Saint Clair, Guy Wenborne (0057)
© Francisco Garcia Huidobro (0058)
0054, (0053)
0055
Makus Wespi Jérôme de Meuron Architekten bsa
www.wespidemeuron.ch
© Makus Wespi Jérôme de Meuron Architekten
0056
Jorge Armando Rodríguez Bello
rodriguezbello2000@yahoo.com
© Jorge Armando Rodríguez Bello
0057, (0053)
0058, (0053)
0059
Nicos Kalogirou
sokinuo@yahoo.com
© Nicos Kalogirou
0060
Europizarras
www.europizarras.net
© Europizarras
0061, 0066, 0341
A-cero Estudio de arquitectura y urbanismo
www.a-cero.com
© Xurxo Lobato (0061)
© Juan Rodríguez, Hisao Suzuki (0066, 0341)
0062, (0017)
0063
Aidlin Darling Design
www.aidlindarlingdesign.com
© John Sutton
0064
Pagani+ Di Mauro Architetti
www.paganidimauro.com
© Andrea Corbellini
0065, (0017)
0066, (0061)
0067, 0068, 0380, 0959
Topos Atelier
www.toposatelier.com
© Xavier Antunes

ellobat@ono.com
© Emilio Llobat Guarino
0135, 0348, 0349
Pascal Arquitectos
www.pascalarquitectos.com
© Víctor Benítez
0136, (0040)
0137, 0354
Stein Halvorsen AS Sivilarkitekter MNAL
www.sh-arkitekter.no
© Kim Müller
0138, 0293
3LHD
www.3lhd.com
© Aljo a Brajdi, 3LHD Archive (0293)
© Damir Fabijani (0138)
0139, 0355, 0420
Studio Giovanni D'Ambrosio
www.giovannidambrosio.com
© Peter Mylonas
0140, (0040)
0141
Atelier Marc Barani
contact@atelierbarani.com
© Serge Demailly
0142, 0377, 0718
Pugh + Scarpa Architects
www.pugh-scarpa.com
© Marvin Rand (0142, 0377)
© Pugh + Scarpa Architects (0718)
0143, 0164, 0216, 0295
Murphy/Jahn Architects
www.murphyjahn.com
© Andreas Keller (0164)
© Doug Snower (0143, 0216)
© H.G. Esch (0295)
0144
© Andreasg/Dreamstime.com
0145, (038)
0146
Ateliers Jean Nouvel, Fermín Vázquez/b720 Arquitectos
www.jeannouvel.fr
www.b720.com
© Òscar García
0147
Guillermo Hevia
www.guillermohevia.cl
© Cristián Barahona, Guillermo Hevia
0148
Hascher und Jehle Architektur
www.hascherjehle.de
© Svenha Bockhop
0149
Fermín Vázquez/b720 Arquitectos
www.b720.com
© Rafael Vargas
0150, (047)
0151, (048)
0152
Brullet-Pineda Arquitectes
www.pinearq.com
© Jordi Miralles
0153
Toyo Ito & Architects Associates, TAISEI Design PAE
www.toyo-ito.co.jp
www.pae.co.jp
© Toyo Ito & Architects Associates, TAISEI Design PAE
0154, 0661
Lazzarini Pickering Architetti
www.lazzarinipickering.com
© Matteo Piazza
0155, 0390
Carlos Ferrater

www.ferrater.com
© Alejo Bagué
0156
India Mahdavi, Javier Sánchez/JSª
www.india-mahdavi.com
www.jsa.com.mx
© Undine Pröhl
0157
Lehrer Architects
www.lehrerarchitects.com
© Marvin Rand
0158, (0128)
0159, (0112)
0160, 0167, 0733
Klein Dytham Architecture
www.klein-dytham.com
© Katsuhisa Kida
0161, (0128)
0162, (079)
0163, 0165, 0171
Steven Holl Architects
www.stevenholl.com
© Andy Ryan
0164, (0143)
0165, (0163)

0166, 0172, 0219, 0720, 0721, 0734, 0744
GMP-Von Gerkan, Marg und Partner Architekten
www.gmp-architekten.de
© Ben McMillan, Christian Gahl (0744)
© Christian Gahl (0166)
© GMP-Von Gerkan, Marg und Partner Architekten (0720, 0721)
© Heiner Leiska (0172)
© Marcus Bredt (0219, 0734)
0167, (0160)
0168, (0017)
0169, (0128)
0170
Galán + Lubascher Arquitectos
www.galanlubascher.com
© Galán + Lubascher Arquitectos
0171, (0163)
0172, (0166)
0173
Michael Singer Studio
www.michaelsinger.com
© Michael Singer
0174, (0020)
0175, (0032)
0176
Dosmasuno Arquitectos
www.dosmasunoarquitectos.com
© Miguel de Guzmán
0177, (0113)
0178, (0117)
0179, 0181
© Anthony Aneese Totah Jr/Dreamstime.com
0180
© Goran Bogicevic/Dreamstime.com
0181, (0179)
0182, (0123)
0183, (0123)
0184
© V. J. Matthew/Dreamstime.com
0185
© Photoclicks/Dreamstime.com
0186, 0482
© William Howell/Dreamstime.com
0187
© Fallsview/Dreamstime.com
0188
© Algimantas Balezentis/Dreamstime.com

0189
© Marek Slusarczyk/Dreamstime.com
0190
© Dan Wallace/Dreamstime.com
0191, 0445
© Ragne Kabanova/Dreamstime.com
0192
Bloomframe
www.bloomframe.com
© Bloomframe
0193
© Risto Hunt/Dreamstime.com
0194, 0223, 0591, 0594
Forjas Artísticas El Francés
www.forja-artistica.es
© Forjas Artísticas El Francés
0195, 0196
Brunete Fraccaroli
www.brunetefraccaroli.com.br
© Rômulo Fialdini (0196)
© Tuca Reinés (0195)
0196, (0195)
0197, 0629
Enric Ruiz-Geli
www.ruiz-geli.com
© Lluís Ros
0198
Nurmela-Raimoranta-Tasa Arkkitehdit
www.n-r-t.f
© Jyriki Tasa, Jussi Tiainen
0199, 0205, 0740
Shuhei Endo Architect Institute
www.paramodern.com
© Toshiraru Kitajima (0740)
© Yoshiharu Matsumura (0199, 0205)
0200
Stefan Sterf Architekten
www.sterfarchitekten.de
© Isabella Scheel
0201
Odden Rodrigues Architects
ora@iinet.net.au
© Robert Frith/Acorn Photo Agency
0202, 0307, 0310
Germán del Sol
www.germandelsol.cl
© Felipe Camus (0202)
© Guy Wemborne (0307, 0310)
0203
Jun Itami Architects
www.junitami.com
© Shigeyuki Morishita
0204, (0128)
0205, (0199)
0206, 0714, 0716, 0751, 0754
ONL-Oosterhuis_Lénárd
ONL-Kas Oosterhuis
www.oosterhuis.nl
© Jeroen Bos/ONL-Oosterhuis_Lénárd (0206)
© ONL-Oosterhuis_Lénárd (0751, 0754)
© Walter Fogel, Festo AG & Co. KG, ONL (0714, 0716)
0207
Jarmund & Vigsnæs Architects
www.jva.no
© Nils Petter Dale
0208, 0737
Sauerbruch Hutton Architects
www.sauerbruchhutton.de
© Gerrit Engel (0208)
© Bitter & Bredt Fotografie (0737)
0209
EMBT – Enric Miralles + Benedetta Tagliabue

0297
© Radomír Rezny/Dreamstime.com
0298, 0633, 0808, 0822
Henning Larsen Architects
www.henninglarsen.com
© Adam Mørk (0298, 0808)
© Henning Larsen Architects (0822)
© Reinhard Görner (0633)
0299, (0083)
0300, 0664
Cecil Balmond/Arup, António Adão-da-Fonseca
www.arup.com
www.adfconsultores.com
© Arup
0301, (0042)
0302, 0366
Site Office Landscape Architecture
www.siteoffice.com.au
© Trevor Mein
0303
Studio Granda Architects
www.studiogranda.is
© Sigurgeir Sigurjónsson
0304, (0021)
0305, (0277)
0306
Rosa Grena Kliass Arquitectura Paisagística
rgkliass@uol.com.br
© Nelson Kon
0307, (0202)
0308, 0370
Carl-Viggo Holmebakk
holmebakk.cvh@getmail.no
© Carl-Viggo Holmebakk, Richard Riesenfeld, Ellen Ane Krog
Eggen, Helge Stikbakke
0309, 0353
Hutterreimann + Cejka Landschaftsarchitekten, Jens Schmahl/
A Lab Arkitektur
www.hr-c.net
www.a-lab.net
© Christo Libuda, Franziska Poreski, Hutterreimann + Cejka
0310, (0202)
0311, (0076)
0312
© Isabel Poulin/Dreamstime.com
0313, (0076)
0314
Damglass
www.damglass.com
© Damglass
0315, (0117)
0316, 0765, 0766, 0769
Agustí Costa
www.agusticosta.com
© David Cardelús
0317
Hideki Yoshimatsu + Archipro Architects
www.archipro.net
© Archipro Architects
0318
SHH Architects
www.shh.co.uk
© SHH Architects
0319, (0074)
0320, 0359
Petr Hájek/HSH architekti
www.hsharchitekti.cz
© Ester Havlová
0321
Carola Vannini Architecture
www.carolavannini.com
© Filippo Vinardi
0322, (0133)

0323, (0017)
0324, (0036)
0325, 0826
Claude Cormier Architectes Paysagistes
www.claudecormier.com
© Claude Cormier Architectes Paysagistes
0326, 0329, 0330, 0331, 0332, 0334, 0336, 0337, 0381, 0382,
0399, 0401, 0402
Maya Romanoff
www.mayaromanoff.com
© Maya Romanoff
0327, (0235)
0328, (0245)
0329, (0326)
0330, (0326)
0331, (0326)
0332, (0326)
0333, 0879
Caramel Architekten, F. Stiper Designer
www.caramel.at
© Caramel Architekten (0333)
© Krems (0879)
0334, (0326)
0335
Mind | Day
www.minday.com
© Larry Gawell
0336, (0326)
0337, (0326)
0338
© Phartisan/Dreamstime.com
0339
Schotten & Hansen
www.schotten-hansen.com
© Schotten & Hansen
0340, 0939
Architecture Project
www.ap.com.mt
© Alberto Favaro
0341, (0061)
0342, 0344, 0346, 0958
Albert Mikoviny
afm.bb@stonline.sk
© Ivan Cilik
0343
Mikhail Olykainen/Dreamstime.com
0344, (0342)
0345, (0235)
0346, (0342)
0347
Mario Botta Architetto
www.botta.ch
© Enrico Cano
0348, (0135)
0349, (0135)
0350, 0369
Jasarevic Architekten
www.b-au.com
© Alen Jasarevic, Angelika Bardehle, Nursen Ozlukurt
0351, 0368
Gregotti Associati International Spa
www.gregottiassociati.it
© Donato di Bello
0352
AREP – Aménagements Recherches Pôles d'Échanges
www.arep.fr
© Pep Escoda
0353, (0309)
0354, (0137)
0355, (0139)
0356, 0371, 0503
Manuel Cervantes Céspedes/CC Arquitectos

www.ccarquitectos.com.mx
© Luis Gordoa
0357
Jeff Brock, Belén Moneo/Moneo Brock Studio
www.moneobrock.com
© Luis Asín, Jeff Brock
0358, (0107)
0359, (0320)
0360, (0234)
0361, (0099)
0362
Álvaro Leite Siza Viera
alvarinhosiza@sapo.pt
© FG + SG
0363, (0079)
0364, (0105)
0365, (0079)
0366, (0302)
0367, (0098)
0368, (0351)
0369, (0350)
0370, (0308)
0371, (0356)
0372, (0047)
0373, 0378, 0421
Juan Carlos Doblado
www.juancarlosdoblado.com
© Alex Kornhuber (0378)
© Elsa Ramírez (0373, 0421)
0374
Felipe Assadi + Francisca Pulido
www.assadi.cl
© Guy Wenborne
0375, (0099)
0376, (0044)
0377, (0142)
0378, (0373)
0379, (0018)
0380, (0067)
0381, (0326)
0382, (0326)
0383
Richard Rogers Partnership, Alonso Balaguer & Arquitectos
Asociados, GCA Arquitectes Associats
www.richardrogers.co.uk
www.alonsobalaguer.com
www.gcaarq.com
© Gogortza & Llorella
0384
RCR Aranda Pigem Vilalta Arquitectes
www.rcrarquitectes.es
© Hisao Suzuki
0385, (0021)
0386
Capella García Arquitectura
www.capellaweb.com
© Rafael Vargas
0387
Jaume Valor
www.exearquitectura.com
© Eugeni Pons
0388
Lluís Clotet, Ignasi Paricio/Clotet, Paricio i Associats
cpa@coac.net
© Lluís Casals
0389, 0702
GCA Arquitectes Associats
www.gcaarq.com
© Jordi Miralles
0390, (0155)
0391, 0392
Josep Lluís Mateo/MAP Architect
www.mateo-maparchitect.com

eat Marugg
finite Light, Beat Marugg
2, (0391)
3
ar Tusquets Blanca
.tusquets.com
unnar Knetchel, Rafael Vargas
4
mann Associates
.lippmann.com.au
ippmann Associates
5
i and Associates
.maki-and-associates.co.jp
hinkenchiku-sha, Toshiharu Kitajima
6, (0108)
7, (0019)
8, (0079)
9, (0326)
0, 0403, 0404
go-Di Palma Associati
.dipalmassociati.com
rtigo-Di Palma Associati
1, (0326)
2, (0326)
3, (0400)
4, (0400)
5, 0408, 0824
t
.graftlab.com
ndi Albert Photographie (0405)
raft (824)
iepler Brunier Architekturfotografie (0408)
6
luse
.vinyluse.com
yniluse
7, (0019)
8, (0405)
9, (0133)
0
ip Xavier Claramunt
.equip.com.es
scer
1, 0412, 0413
m Ceramica
.arkim.it
rkim Ceramica
2, (0411)
3, (0411)
4
rici cerámica y porcelánico
.aparici.com
Aparici
5, (0133)
6, (0133)
17, 0659
ssmann_de Bruyn
.cossmann-debruyn.de
Nicole Zimmermann
8, (0133)
9
dau & Kindelbacher Architekten Innerarchitekten
.landaukindelbacher.de
Christian Hacker
20, (0139)
21, (0373)
22, (0108)
23, (0008)
24
ibos Studis

dal@coac.net
© Miquel Tres
0425, 0426
Barry Sugerman
www.barrysugerman.com
© Pep Escoda
0426, (0425)
0427, (0118)
0428, (0117)
0429, (0078)
0430, (0032)
0431
© Vinicius Tupinamba/Dreamstime.com
0432, 0433
Ian Ayers & Francesc Zamora
ianayers@gmail.com
© Francesc Zamora
0433, (0432)
0434
Matali Crasset
www.matalicrasset.com
© Patrick Gries
0435, (0434)
0436
Die Baupiloten
www.baupiloten.com
© Jan Bitter
0437
Hofman Dujardin Architectuur
www.hofmandujardin.nl
© Matthijs von Roon
0438
Burkhalter Sumi architekten
www.burkhalter-sumi.ch
© Heinz Unger
0439, 0442
Alonso Balaguer y Arquitectos Asociados
www.alonsobalaguer.com
© Alonso Balaguer y Arquitectos Asociados
0440, (0118)
0441
Vidal y Asociados Arquitectos
www.luisvidal.com
© Ignacio Álvarez Monteserín
0442, (0439)
0443, 0563
© Loft Publications
0444, (0245)
0445, (0191)
0446, (0133)
0447
© Stephen Coburn/Dreamstime.com
0448, 0456, 0463, 0467
© Baloncici/Dreamstime.com
0449
© Benis Arapovic/Dreamstime.com
0450
© Igor Terekhov/Dreamstime.com
0451
© Yulia Saponova/Dreamstime.com
0452, 0906
© Nick Stubbs/Dreamstime.com
0453, (0245)
0454, (0245)
0455
© Gemenacom/Dreamstime.com
0456, (0448)
0457
© Igorr/Dreamstime.com
0458
© Thorsten/Dreamstime.com
0459
© Darryl Brooks/Dreamstime.com

0460
© Joe Gough/Dreamstime.com
0461
© Piotr Antonów/Dreamstime.com
0462
© Vuk Vukoslavovic/Dreamstime.com
0463, (0448)
0464
© Serdabarsak/Dreamstime.com
0465
© Ryby/Dreamstime.com
0466
© Ken Toh/Dreamstime.com
0467, (0448)
0468
© Norman Chan/Dreamstime.com
0469
© Rod He/Dreamstime.com
0470, (0255)
0471, 0572
Seno & Siffredi/Colpi di Martello
www.colpidimartello.it
© Seno & Siffredi/Colpi di Martello
0472
Tino & Ricardo Barbosa/Barbosa Space Projects
www.barbosasp.com
© Marce Sedano
0473, 0597
Johan Cubillos/Hierro Ornamental
www.johancubillos.com
© Johan Cubillos/Hierro Ornamental
0474, (0255)
0475, 0481, 0568, 0583, 0584, 0585, 0586, 0587, 0588, 0595
Scarsi Bernardo S.n.c.
www.scarsibernardo.com
© Virginia Scarsi
0476, (0222)
0477
Ibarra Rosano Design Architects
www.ibarrarosano.com
© Ibarra Rosano Design Architects
0478
© Lucabertolli/Dreamstime.com
0479
© Pavalache Stelian/Dreamstime.com
0480
© VVoronov/Dreamstime.com
0481, (0475)
0482, (0186)
0483
© Josef Muellek/Dreamstime.com
0484
© Mohamed Badawi/Dreamstime.com
0485
BOB361 Architects
www.bob361.com
© Nullens André
0486
CLE Architects Limited
www.cl3.com
© CLE Architects Limited
0487, (0128)
0488
Fougeron Architects
www.fougeron.com
© Richard Barnes
0489
© Petr Vaclavek/Dreamstime.com
0490, 0558
Architekten Tillner & Willinger

www.tw-arch.at
© Architekten Tillner & Willinger
0491
Lemonpack
www.lemonpack.com
© Lemonpack
0492, 0642
La Dallman
www.ladallman.com
© Kevin J. Miyazaki
0493, (0018)
0494
Sevasa
www.sevasa.com
© CriSamar® STEP
0495, (0023)
0496
Ateliers Jean Nouvel
www.jeannouvel.com
© Pep Escoda
0497
Tony Trobe/TT Architecture
www.ttarchitecture.com.au
© Tony Trobe
0498
Lichtblau + Wagner Architekten
www.lichtblauwagner.com
© Bruno Klomfar
0499
HOK- Hellmuth, Obata + Kassabaum
www.hok.com
© HOK- Hellmuth, Obata + Kassabaum
0500, (0111)
0501, 0821
KPMB Architects, GBCA Architects
www.kpmbarchitects.com
www.gbca.ca
© Eduard Heuber/Arch Photo, Tom Arban/Tom Arban
Photography
0502
© Yuri Strakhov/Dreamstime.com
0503, (0356)
0504, 0818
KPMB Architects
www.kpmbarchitects.com
© Eduard Heuber/Arch Photo, Marc Cramer, Tom Arban/Tom
Arban Photography
0505
Jan Søndergaard/KHR Arkitekter AS
www.khr.dk
© Ib Sørensen
0506
Theo Hotz Architekten + Planer AG
www.theohotz.ch
© Rolf Gähwiler
0507
© Jose Gil/Dreamstime.com
0508, 0509, 0538, 0554
© Joanne Zh/Dreamstime.com
0509, (0508)
0510
© Melinda Fawver/Dreamstime.com
0511, (0220)
0512, 0525
© Branislav Senic/Dreamstime.com
0513
© Tomasz Markowski/Dreamstime.com
0514
© Jorge Salcedo/Dreamstime.com
0515
© Rangerx/Dreamstime.com
0516

© Judy Ben Joud/Dreamstime.com
0517, (0218)
0518
© Davidmartyn/Dreamstime.com
0519
© Elena Elisseeva/Dreamstime.com
0520
© Sparkia/Dreamstime.com
0521
© Krzysztof Korolonek/Dreamstime.com
0522
© Fred Goldstein/Dreamstime.com
0523
© Marjan Veljanoski/Dreamstime.com
0524
© Bosenok/Dreamstime.com
0525, (0512)
0526, (0220)
0527
© Lance Bellers/Dreamstime.com
0528
© Vangelis/Dreamstime.com
0529
© Startoucher/Dreamstime.com
0530
© Yali Shi/Dreamstime.com
0531
© Photawa/Dreamstime.com
0532
© Natalia Guseva/Dreamstime.com
0533
© Drbouz/Dreamstime.com
0534, 0541
© Kheng Guan Toh/Dreamstime.com
0535
© Peter Albrektsen/Dreamstime.com
0536
© Italianestro/Dreamstime.com
0537
© Frode Krogstad/Dreamstime.com
0538, (0508)
0539
© Mirage1/Dreamstime.com
0540
© Lawrence Wee/Dreamstime.com
0541, (0534)
0542
© Maxim Petrichuk/Dreamstime.com
0543
© Videowokart/Dreamstime.com
0544
© Steve Lovegrove/Dreamstime.com
0545
© Photoblueice/Dreamstime.com
0546
© Andrei Radzkou/Dreamstime.com
0547, 0904
© Joan Coll Jcvstock/Dreamstime.com
0548
© Krzyssagit/Dreamstime.com
0549
© Svlumagraphica/Dreamstime.com
0550
© Andris Piebalgs/Dreamstime.com
0551
© Felix Chen/Dreamstime.com
0552
© Lennyfdzz/Dreamstime.com
0553
© Lucy Cherniak/Dreamstime.com

0554, (0508)
0555, (0112)
0556, 0682, 0760
Nieberg Architect
www.nieberg-architect.de
© Nieberg Architect
0557
© Jasmin Krpan/Dreamstime.com
0558, (0490)
0559, (0032)
0560, (0112)
0561, (0112)
0562, (0039)
0563, (0443)
0564
© David Morgan/Dreamstime.com
0565, (0008)
0566
Metalunic
www.metalunic.com
© Metalunic
0567, (0222)
0568, (0475)
0569, 0570, 0573, 0575, 0576, 0578, 0579, 0581, 0582, 0585
0590, 0593, 0596, 0598
© Miquel Xirau
0570, (0569)
0571
Fibo Leuchten-Schmiedeeisen
www.fibo-leuchten.de
© Fibo Leuchten-Schmiedeeisen
0572, (0471)
0573, (0569)
0574
Ricardo Cabrera/Artesano Iron Works
www.artesanoironworks.com
© Artesano Iron Works
0575, (0569)
0576, (0569)
0577, 0592
Santi Fuchs/Arte-Sano
www.arte-sano.net
© Santi Fuchs/Arte-Sano
0578, (0569)
0579, (0569)
0580, (0255)
0581, (0569)
0582, (0569)
0583, (0475)
0584, (0475)
0585, (0475)
0586, (0475)
0587, (0475)
0588, (0475)
0589, (0569)
0590, (0194)
0591, (0194)
0592, (0577)
0593, (0569)
0594, (0194)
0595, (0475)
0596, (0569)
0597, (0473)
0598, (0569)
0599, 0600
Unopiù
www.unopiu.it
© Unopiù
0600, (0599)
0601, 0605, 0607
Bloch Design

0681, (0111)
0682, (0556)
0683, (0117)
0684, 0686
Foscarini
www.foscarini.com
© Foscarini
0685, 0792, 0793, 0798, 0802, 0806
One Plus Partnership
www.onepluspartnership.com
© Gabriel Leung (0792, 0793, 0798, 0802)
© Law Ling Kit, Virginia Lung (0685, 0806)
0686, (0684)
0687, (0111)
0688
Hild und K Architekten
www.hildundk.de
© Hild und K Architekten
0689, (0253)
0690, (0074)
0691, (0023)
0692, (0074)
0693, (0222)
0694
United Visual Artists, Onepointsix
www.uva.co.uk
www.onepointsix.co.uk
© United Visual Artists
0695, 0845, 0867
Michelle Kaufmann Designs
www.mkd-arc.com
© Michelle Kaufmann Designs (0867)
© John Swain (0695, 0845)
0696, (0637)
0697, 0853, 0859
Luis de Garrido
www.luisdegarrido.com
© David Campos, Habitat Futura (0697)
© Maite Piera (0853)
© Luis de Garrido (0859)
0698, 0736, 0882
NMDA – Neil M. Denari Architects
www.nmda-inc.com
© NMDA-Neil M. Denari Architects
0699, 0841
Luca Lancini/FUJY
www.lucalancini.com
© Miguel de Guzmán
0700, 0872, 0875
Jeremy Edmiston, Douglas Gauthier/System Architects
www.systemarchitects.net
© Jeremy Edmiston, Douglas Gauthier/System Architects
0701, 0719
Atelier Tekuto
www.tekuto.com
© Atelier Tekuto
0702, (0389)
0703, 0825
Chris Bosse
www.chrisbosse.com
© Chris Bosse
0704
1+2 Architecture
www.1plus2architecture.com
© 1+2 Architecture
0705
Brauen + Waelchli Arquitecture
www.bw-arch.ch
© Thomas Jantscher, Jean-Philippe Daulte
0706, 0829, 0831
Griffin Enright Architects
www.griffinenrightarchitects.com

© Benny Chan (0706)
© Griffin Enright Architects (0829, 0831)
0707, 0709, 0812
Studio 63 Architecture & Design
www.studio63.it
© Rimini Fiera-SIA Guest (0813)
© Yael Pincus (0707, 0709)
0708
PTW Architects
www.ptw.com.au
© PTW Architects
0709, (0707)
0710
Paul Cocksedge Studio
www.paulcocksedge.co.uk
© Richard Brine
0711, 0712
Ximena Muñoz, Mónica Labra, Rodrigo Gajardo, Paulina Villalobos,
Stefano Benaglia/theANEMIX
www.theanemix.com
© www.kerbe.com.uk, Ximena Muñoz
0712, (0711)
0713
Masamichi Udagawa & Sigi Moeslinger/Antenna Design
www.antennadesign.com
© Ryuzo Masunaga
0714, (0206)
0715
Peter Marino
www.petermarinoarchitect.com
© Peter Marino, Takashi Orii, Vincent Kapp
0716, (0206)
0717, 0835
Kramm & Strigl
www.kramm-strigl.de
© Dieter Leistner, Kramm Strigl
0718, (0142)
0719, (0701)
0720, (0166)
0721, (0166)
0722
Cannatà & Fernandes Arquitectos
www.cannatafernandes.com
© Luís Ferreira Alves
0723, (0038)
0724, (0235)
0725, (0637)
0726, (0285)
0727, (0625)
0728
Céline Michaux Architectes Associés
www.cmarchi.be
© Céline Michaux Architectes Associés
0729
Ofis Arhitekti
www.ofis-a.si
© Toma Gregori
0730
Romain Brenas & Rémy Casteu
www.brenas.fr
© Romain Brenas & Rémy Casteu
0731, (0090)
0732
Strobl Architekten
www.stroblarchitekten.at
© Josefine Unterhauser
0733, (0160)
0734, (0166)
0735, 0745
David Randall Hertz/SEA – Studio of Enviromental Architecture
www.studioea.com
© Jeurgen Nogai

0736, (0698)
0737, (0208)
0738, 0753
Manuelle Gautrand
www.manuelle-gautrand.com
© Manuelle Gautrand (0753)
© Philippe Ruault, Platform (0738)
0739, (0213)
0740, (0199)
0741, (0010)
0742, (0213)
0743
Nicholas Grimshaw & Partners
www.grimshaw-architects.com
© Nicholas Grimshaw & Partners
0744, (0166)
0745, (0735)
0746, (0079)
0747, (0128)
0748, 0749
Zwarts & Jansma Architects
www.zwarts.jansma.nl
© DigiDaan
© Zwarts & Jansma Architects
0749, (0748)
0750, 0945
Plajer & Franz
www.plajer-franz.de
© www.diephotodesigner.de
0751, (0206)
0752
Frank Gehry
www.foga.com
© Adrian Tyler
0753, (0738)
0754, (0206)
0755, (0079)
0756
3DELUXE transdiciplinary design
www.3deluxe.com
© 3DELUXE transdiciplinary design
0757
Obra Architects
www.obraarchitects.com
© Obra Architects
0758, (0248)
0759, (0019)
0760, (0556)
0761
Behles & Jochimsen
www.behlesjochimsen.de
© Marcus Bredt
0762
Realarchitektur
www.realarchitektur.de
© Martin Widerberg
0763, (0250)
0764
© Stratum/Dreamstime.com
0765, (0316)
0766, (0316)
0767
Molteni
www.molteni.it
© Molteni
0768
Desalto
www.desalto.it
© Desalto
0769, (0316)
0770, 0772
Tom Allisma Productions

www.arkintilt.com
© Arkin Tilt Architects
0850
Ray Kappe + DU Architects
www.kappedu.com
© Ray Kappe
0851
Studio 804
www.studio804.com
© Studio 804
0852, (0644)
0853, (0697)
0854
Sebastián Irarrázaval
www.sebastianirarrazaval.com
© Carlos Eguiguren
0855
Pich-Aguilera
www.picharchitects.com
© Pich-Aguilera
0856
Sambuichi Architects
samb@d2.dion.ne.jp
© Hiroyuki Hirai
0857
Atelier Werner Schmidt
www.atelierwernerschmidt.ch
© Atelier Werner Schmidt
0858, 0860
Belzberg Architects
www.belzbergarchitects.com
© Benny Chan/Fotoworks, Belzberg Architects
0859, (0697)
0860, (0858)
0861, 0863
SSD Architecture + Urbanism
www.ssdarchitecture.com
© SSD Architecture + Urbanism
0862
RAU
www.rau.eu
© Kusters fotografie
0863, (0861)
0864
Vastu Shilpa Consultants
www.sangath.org
© Vastu Shilpa Consultants
0865
MITHUN architects+designers+planners
www.mithun.com
© JH
0866, 0871
Erin Moore
eemoore@u.arizona.edu
© Gary Tarleton
0867, (0695)
0868
Stefan Eberstadt
stefan.eberstadt@stefaneberstadt.de
© Stefan Eberstadt
0869
Jennifer Siegal/Office of Mobile Design
www.designmobile.com
© Jennifer Siegal/Office of Mobile Design
0870, 0877, 0885
Andrew Maynard Architects
www.maynardarchitects.com
© Andrew Maynard Architects
0871, (0866)
0872, (0700)
0873, (0625)
0874
Olgga Architects

www.olgga.fr
© Olgga Architects
0875, (0700)
0876
DeMaria Design Associates
www.demariadesign.com
© Andre Movsesyan, Christian Kienapfel
0877, (0870)
0878, (0883)
Ecosistema Urbano
www.ecosistemaurbano.org
© Emilio P. Doiztua
0879, (0333)
0880
Arquitectura X
www.arquitecturax.com
© Arquitectura X
0881
Andrade Morettin Associated Architects
www.andrademorettin.com.br
© Andrade Morettin Associated Architects
0882, (0698)
0883, (0878)
0884
Hobby A.Schuster & Maul, Gerold Peham
www.nomadhome.com
© Marc Haader
0885, (0870)
0886
Holzbox
www.holzbox.at
© Holzbox
0887
© Tom Dowd/Dreamstime.com
0888
© Robert Lerich/Dreamstime.com
0889
© António Nunes/Dreamstime.com
0890
© Gira/Dreamstime.com
0891
© Alex Bramwell/Dreamstime.com
0892
© Bertrandb/Dreamstime.com
0893, 0907
© Colleen Coombe/Dreamstime.com
0894
© Saporob/Dreamstime.com
0895
© Lars Christensen/Dreamstime.com
0896
© Nikolay Okhitin/Dreamstime.com
0897
© Denis Kartavenko/Dreamstime.com
0898
© Youssouf Cader/Dreamstime.com
0899
© Deshacam/Dreamstime.com
0900
© Knud Nielsen/Dreamstime.com
0901
© Juanjo Tugores/Dreamstime.com
0902
© Natalia Vasina Vladimirovna/Dreamstime.com
0903, (0260)
0904, (0547)
0905, (0260)
0906, (0452)
0907, (0893)
0908, 0911, 0914, 0916, 0928
JML Arquitectura del Agua

www.jeanmaxllorca.com
© Stephane Llorca
0909, 0910, 0933
Pete O'Shea ASLA FAAR/Siteworks Studio
www.siteworks-studio.com
© Pete O'Shea ASLA FAAR/Siteworks Studio
0910, (0909)
0911, (0908)
0912
Thilo Folkerts, SPAX architects
www.tfolkerts.de
www.spax.cc
© Sébastien Secchi
0913, 0919, 0983
SLA Landskabsarkitekter
www.sla.dk
© Frode Birk Nielsen (0919)
© SLA, Jens Lindhe, Lars Bahl, Torben Petersen (0913)
© Torben Petersen (0983)
0914, (0908)
0915, 0963, 0965, 0966
Delta Vorm Groep
www.deltavormgroep.nl
© Frank Colder, Picture7
0916, (0908)
0917, 0918, 0949
Atelier Dreiseitl
www.dreiseitl.de
© Atelier Dreiseitl
0918, (0917)
0919, (0913)
0920, 0986, 0987
NIPpaysage
www.nippaysage.ca
© NIPpaysage
0921, 0998
Turenscape
www.turenscape.com
© Cao Yang, Kongjian Yu
0922
Paolo L. Bürgi/Studio Bürgi
www.burgi.ch
© Paolo L. Bürgi/Studio Bürgi
0923, 0995
Dal Pian Arquitetos Associados
www.dalpian.arq.br
© Dal Pian Arquitetos Associados
0924
Lorenzo Castro
lcastroj@unal.edu.co
© Guillermo Quintero, Sergio García, Ana María Pradilla, Lorenz
Castro
0925, 0992
Scapelab
www.scapelab.com
© Miran Kambic
0926
TEAM Landschaftsarchitekten – Winterthur
www.team-landschaft.ch
© Hansjorg Walter
0927
Birk Nielsens Tegnestue
www.birknielsen.dk
© Frode Birk Nielsen
0928, (0908)
0929
Buro Sant en Co
www.santenco.nl
© Buro Sant en Co
0930
Raymond Jungles Landscape Architecture

.raymondjungles.com
enny Provo
1
ner & Chapman Landscape Design
.faulknerchapman.com.au
nania Sheguedyn
2
delet
.dardelet.ch
ardelet
3, (0909)
4
afson Porter
/.gustafson-porter.com
ustafson Porter
5
t 8 Urban Design & Landscape Architecture
v.west8.nl
Vest 8 Urban Design & Landscape Architecture
6, (0017)
7
hak
v.pushak.no
ushak
8
hoeven CS
w.venhoevencs.nl
enhoeven CS
9, (0340)
0
cis Vermonden
monden@gmail.com
rancis Vermonden
1, (0281)
2
en Fortune
w.greenfortune.com
Green Fortune
3, (0106)
4
enmeme
w.greenmeme.com
Greenmeme
5, (0750)
6
he Richter Teherani Architekten
w.brt.de
Thomas Jantscher
7
orsanger Architects
w.voorsanger.com
Thomas Damgaard
8
teich/J. N. Jardins Naturels
w.bioteich.fr
Erick Saillet
9, (0917)
50
rick Blanc
w.murvegetalpatrickblanc.com
Patrick Blanc
51
nes Corner Field Operations, Diller Scofidio+Renfro
w.fieldoperations.net
w.dillerscofidio.com
James Corner Field Operations, Diller Scofidio+Renfro
52
eehouse Company
w.treehousecompany.com
Chris Tubbs
53
exander Oesterheld
w.die-gartenidee.de

© Ferdinand Graf von Luckner
0954, (0107)
0955, (0257)
0956
Kiyoshi Sey Takeyama/AMORPHE
www.amorphe.jp
© Koichi Torimura
0957
Minsuk Cho + Kisu Park/Mass Studies
www.massstudies.com
© Yong-Kwan Kim
0958, (0342)
0959, (0067)
0960, (0289)
0961
Levin Monsigny Landscape Architects
levin.monsigny@yahoo.de
© Claas Dreppenstedt
0962, 0985
Rush & Wright Associates
www.rushwright.com
© Derek Swalwell, Peter Bennetts (0985)
© Peter Clarke (0962)
0963, (0915)
0964
Atelier Le Balto
www.lebalto.de
© Yann Monel
0965, (0915)
0966, (0915)
0967, 0968
GROSS. MAX. Landscape Architects
www.grossmax.com
© GROSS. MAX., Mark Dion
0968, (0967)
0969
West & Partner
www.west-partner.ch
© West & Partner
0970
Landworks Studio
www.landworks-studio.com
© Landworks Studio
0971
Orlando Busarello, Dilva Cândida, Daniela Slomp Busarello
www.slompbusarello.com.br
© Slomp & Busarello Architects
0972
Satoshi Okada Architects
www.okada-archi.com
© Satoshi Okada Architects
0973
Koseli ka Landschaftsarchitektur
www.koselicka.at
© Koseli ka Landschaftsarchitektur
0974
TOPOTEK 1 landscape architects
www.topotek1.de
© Hanns Joosten
0975
Daniela Moderini, Laura Zampieri, Ippolito Pizetti
www.moderini.com
© Daniela Moderini, Laura Zampieri, Ippolito Pizetti
0976, (0279)
0977
Groep Delta Architectuur
www.groepdelta.com
© Groep Delta Architectuur
0978
Andrea Cochran
www.acochran.com
© Andrea Cochran
0979, (0117)

0980, (0038)
0981, (0117)
0982
Burger Landschaftsarchitekten
www.burgerlandschaftsarchitekten.de
© Burger Landschaftsarchitekten, Florian Holzherr, Rakete
0983, (0913)
0984
John Cunningham Architects, Landworks Studio, Office DA
jcarchinc@aol.com
www.landworks-studio.com
www.officeda.com
© Landworks Studio
0985, (0962)
0986, (0920)
0987, (0920)
0988
Oslund and Associates
www.oaala.com
© George Heinrich
0989
Taylor Cullity Lethlean
www.tcl.net.au
© Ben Wrigley, Carla Gottgens
0990, (0662)
0991
De Amicis Architetti
www.deamicisarchitetti.it
© De Amicis Architetti
0992, (0925)
0993, (0675)
0994
LAND-I Archicolture
www.archicolture.com
© Roberto Capecci, Raffaella Sini
0995, (0923)
0996
Carlos Martínez Architekten, Pipilotti Rist/Hauser & Wirth
www.carlosmartinez.ch
www.pipilottirist.net
© Hannes Thalmann, Marc Wetli
0997
Urbanus Architecture & Design
www.urbanus.com.cn
© Yan Meng, Jiu Chen
0998, (0921)
0999
Toyo Ito & Architects Associates, JML Arquitectura del Agua
www.toyo-ito.co.jp
www.jeanmaxllorca.com
© Stéphane Llorca
1,000
Donaldson & Warn Architects
www.donaldsonandwarn.com.au
© Martin Farquharson